Small Trees
for the Tropical
Landscape

Small Trees for the Tropical Landscape

A GARDENER'S GUIDE

Fred D. Rauch

Paul R. Weissich

University of Hawai'i Press
Honolulu

© 2009 University of Hawai'i Press
All rights reserved
Printed in China
14 13 12 11 10 09   6 5 4 3 2 1

Library of Congress Cataloging-in-Publication Data
Rauch, Fred D. (Fred Donald), 1931–
Small trees for the tropical landscape : a gardener's guide /
Fred D. Rauch and Paul R. Weissich.
    p. cm.
Includes bibliographical references and index.
ISBN 978-0-8248-3308-4 (hard cover : alk. paper)
    1. Trees in cities — Tropics.   2. Ornamental trees —
Tropics.   3. Urban forestry — United States.
I. Weissich, Paul R.   II. Title.
SB436.R38   2009
635.9'770913 — dc22   2008049086

University of Hawai'i Press books are printed on acid-free
paper and meet the guidelines for permanence and durability
of the Council on Library Resources

Designed by April Leidig-Higgins

Printed by Everbest Printing Co., Ltd.

Contents

Acknowledgments

The authors are indebted to the following for providing special professional information or services: Frankie Sekiya; Don Hodel: photos of *Plumeria obtusa* (Bahamas) (habit and close-up), *Plumeria obtusa* var. *sericifolia* (habit), *Pterocarpus rohrii* (habit), *Hibiscus arnottianus* subsp. *immaculatus* and *Lysiloma bahamensis* (flower close-ups), *Schefflera elegantissima*, and *Graptophyllum pictum* (habit); Keith Leber: *Parmentiera cerifera* (trunk with fruit); Leland Miyano; Dr. and Mrs. Albert Yellin; Larry Yoshida; Nathan Wong; James Little; the staffs of the National Tropical Botanical Garden, Honolulu Botanical Gardens, Lyon Arboretum, Waimea Arboretum and Botanical Garden, and the Amy Greenwell Ethnobotanical Garden; the Friends of Honolulu Botanical Gardens; Mr. and Mrs. Lelan Nishek and staff of the Kauai Nursery and Landscaping Co.; and the authors of *Nā Lei Makamae*, Marie A. McDonald and Paul R. Weissich, for permission to use the following photographs from that publication: *Kokia drynarioides*, *Metrosideros tremuloides* (close-ups of flowers), and *Pandanus tectorius* (close-up of *hīnano*, the male inflorescence). Honolulu graphic artist David Swann produced the pruning sketches on page 126. Dr. Fred Rauch is responsible for all photography with the exceptions noted above.

Introduction

During the past several decades the American cityscape has seen radical changes. Large areas have been cleared of natural vegetation to accommodate new residential subdivisions, shopping malls, freeways, and airports. Condominiums and large apartment complexes have proliferated, replacing single family residential areas. Streets have been widened to allow for greatly increased traffic flow and the installation of new utility lines. The large trees once shading these streets have been removed. As a result, the "Urban Forest"—consisting of all city trees natural and planted—has been severely and negatively impacted.

The Urban Forest provides major services to the community. In addition to enhancing our quality of life through beautifying our gardens, parks, playgrounds, and roadsides, trees reduce water runoff and erosion and augment the seeping of water into the aquifer. Trees produce oxygen, absorb carbon dioxide and gaseous pollutants, trap particulates, and reduce summer temperatures. Those with pulmonary and cardiovascular problems fare better in air "cleaned" by trees. In fact, we are all benefited, although there are a few of us who react unfavorably to certain seasonal pollens and other tree products.

In February 2003, Dr. Michael. P. Dombeck, former chief of the U.S. Forest Service, published a study in the *Chicago Tribune* indicating that we are losing four trees through clearing and grading for every tree planted in real estate and other land developments. This is a wake-up call for the critical need that exists for greatly increased planting in the Urban Forest and the need to popularize small trees appropriate for planting in diminished urban landscape spaces.

Small Trees for the Tropical Landscape lists 129 species and subspecies and 48 named varieties, cultivars, and forms, plus 23 hybrids appropriate for the home garden and for confined public landscape spaces unable to accommodate larger-growing species formerly in common use. They all contribute to the total of urban ecological, health, and beautification benefits enhancing our lives. "Small trees" are defined as those that—under optimal horticultural practices—may grow up to approximately 30 feet in height. Variation must be expected, however, due to soil and rainfall differences and to the level of care provided by the gardener. Also, many references frequently vary widely in recording heights, which may be attributed to environmental differences and/or clonal variation. The authors' practical, local experience has been a major factor in listing appropriate small trees.

We have included several species that, in time, will or may grow to a greater height than that of our definition of a small tree. The tree, however, will probably stay within our height limit for the life of the garden or the life of its gardener. In each case, these have been so noted. These are highly useful species and should not, in the view of the authors, be ignored.

The second portion of the text, "Tailored Small Trees," beginning on page 126, is rather unorthodox but very useful for the small property. It recommends the planting of large shrubs to be used in the Urban Forest—shrubs that may be readily transformed into appropriate small trees or "tailored trees" through intelligent, selective pruning. This special section lists sixty-eight species and subspecies, forty named varieties and cultivars and forms, and twenty-one hybrids that are appropriate for this conversion.

This publication is in compliance with the Hawai'i-Pacific Weed Risk Assessment Project (HPWRA). See Appendix A.

Plant Names

Trees are listed alphabetically by genus. For the most part, the scientific names are those appearing in *A Tropical Garden Flora* by Dr. George W. Staples and Dr. Derral R. Herbst. Other taxonomic and descriptive resources are listed in the bibliography. Every effort has been made to obtain the most current correct plant name. Errors are the sole responsibility of the authors. Common names for plants vary widely throughout the world. Those most commonly used in Hawai'i, plus Hawaiian plant names where appropriate, have been selected. Where no common name was found, we have taken the liberty of suggesting one.

Plant Selection

The following are helpful guidelines for the selection of the best small tree for the home landscape, condominium/apartment complexes, and public areas with restricted landscape spaces:

1. Determine the function of the small tree: to shade a walkway, as foundation planting, as a focal point, for screening or windbreak, and so forth;

2. Determine desired characteristics such as height (within the range offered), color of foliage, or flowers;

3. List your site's environmental characters: rainfall, wind exposure and amount of sunshine (both problems are complicated by high-rise structures), salt air exposure, and soil quality;

4. List possible negative considerations (toxic sap, thorns, allergies, excessive leaf or fruit fall)

5. Use the tree guide to match landscape needs toward making selections providing minimal maintenance and maximum satisfaction.

Several appendices at the end of this guide will serve to assist the gardener with selection. A list of references provides sources of information that will greatly augment the gardener's understanding and appreciation of small tropical trees.

A Word to the Wise Gardener

Plants produce a wide range of chemical substances as well as physical properties that must be considered in making small tree selections. Some have thorns, irritating hairs or sap, and even poisons that may create problems if not recognized and dealt with. Of major concern to parents are plants that contain toxins that might be fatal to small children. Reactions vary from adult person to adult person and from child to child depending on the amount of exposure and body weight. Teach your children not to smell, pick, and—especially—ingest leaves and flowers. To be certain, stress that ALL leaves and flowers are to be avoided—not touched, chewed, or swallowed. Those species in the text that may pose problems are marked as follows: (T) after the common name indicates the presence of thorns; (S) indicates species known to have caused skin, eye, mouth, or throat irritations; (P) indicates plants with toxic sap, leaves, flowers, or seeds; and (+) indicates plants deserving extra care when handling.

Nitrogen Fixing

A number of plants have the ability to absorb nitrogen from the atmosphere and convert it to a form available to the plant in the soil. This is a great advantage in the garden. In the plant lists that follow, nitrogen fixers are noted by the addition of (N) following the common name. (NP) indicates that other species of the same genus are listed as nitrogen fixers, and there is a high probability that this species is also a nitrogen fixer.

Small Trees for the Tropical Landscape

Acnistis arborescens

Gallinero
Solanaceae (Potato Family)

A small tree growing slowly to 20 feet in height, this species develops a fissured, corky bark that is an excellent site for the hobbyist-grower to display his collection of small epiphytic ferns, bromeliads, and orchids. Its yellowish flowers are inconspicuous. Branching is rather vertical, forming an open canopy. Minor pruning may enhance its shape. Plant it in full sun in an open, well-drained soil. Moderate watering is recommended. Its native lands include the islands of the Caribbean, Mexico, and south to Peru and Brazil. It provides a pleasant, open shade and is well used to line both sides of a walkway in a narrow space. Gallinero is moderately wind tolerant but will not tolerate drought or salt.

Note: A number of genera and species of the Potato Family (formerly called the Nightshade Family) contain toxic substances. Always maintain care when handling.

Amherstia nobilis
Amherstia (N)
Fabaceae (Bean Family)

Flowers of a striking pink with a yellow spot are borne in long pendant racemes on this delicate tree from Myanmar. New foliage is pendant, a colorful purplish turning green, and becoming erect upon maturity. Amherstia must be planted in the light shade of a larger cover tree. It must have protection from wind. A rich, well-drained, moist soil will produce good but slow growth. Amherstia will reach 30 feet in height, although some authors ascribe a greater height. It is considered one of the jewels of tropical trees and produces a striking color accent and focal point for the garden.

Anacardium occidentale
Cashew Nut Tree (P) (S)
Anacardiaceae (Cashew Family)

Growing to 30 feet, this drought-, wind-, and salt-tolerant tree is native to tropical America. It is best known from dry areas of coastal northeastern Brazil. It bears attractive foliage on a wide-spreading crown, in addition to the popular but toxic cashew nut. Great care must be taken to process the fruit, which is high in essential vitamins. Avoid handling the fruit without hand protection, as juice from around the shell may cause irritation on susceptible skin. Many gardeners eat the delicious, nontoxic, red fleshy fruit base and discard the nut itself. It is a moderately slow grower. Use this tree for its fruit, as a windbreak, as a small shade tree, and for the reddish color of its new foliage. It is recommended for the beach garden and xeriscape.

Annona muricata

Soursop (P)
Annonaceae (Custard Apple Family)

Prized for its large fruit used to make a delicious sherbet, for its juice, or eaten as a dessert fruit, this tropical American tree will reach 20 feet in height. There are several improved selections, including 'Dulce' and 'Fiberless Cuban'. A moderate grower, it produces best in a well-drained, moist soil with regular watering and feeding. It will tolerate moderate wind but not salt or drought. Its shape is enhanced by careful pruning. Soursop seeds are reputedly toxic. Another species of *Annona* is a popular landscape subject: Sugar Apple (*Annona squamosa*). It grows to 20 feet in height and is another tropical American tree whose fruit is eaten fresh or made into a refreshing beverage or to flavor ice cream. It requires a well-drained soil but tolerates a wide range of soils and is moderately salt and wind resistant. A hybrid, *Annona* x *atemoya*, called Atemoya, has similar size and growth requirements as the species and is thought by some to produce a superior-tasting fruit.

A. squamosa

A. x *atemoya*

Archidendron clypearia

Archidendron
Fabaceae (Bean Family)

Evergreen, delicate, dark green foliage forming a rounded canopy to 30 feet in height marks this species as a good candidate for the small tree list. White, fuzzy flowers, much like a small powder puff, and many twisted, bright orange-red fruits complete the ornamental character of this tree from high rainfall areas of north India east to southeastern Asia, New Guinea, and the Philippines. Flowers appear in late winter, the colorful seed pods following in early spring. Plant it in full sun in a rich, well-drained loam. This species is moderately slow growing. It requires regular watering. It shows no tolerance of drought or salt but is moderately tolerant of wind. In addition to its pleasant, light shade, it finds use as an unusual color accent against a light-colored wall or tall, light green background plants.

Averrhoa carambola

Carambola, Star Fruit
Oxalidaceae (Wood-Sorrel Family)

This small Malaysian tree reaches 25 feet in height and is a moderately rapid grower. It is valued for its fruit, which may be carried several times a year but in profusion in summer. Selections such as 'Kajang' and 'Kary'are excellent. Plant Carambola where its plentiful fruit may be easily picked. It does best in full sun in a rich, well-drained soil with regular watering. Its drooping branches may require moderate pruning to lift the crown, especially when fruit laden. Its dense crown makes it a useful screening species. Fruit trees such as Carambola are a source of highly desirable fruit, but be aware that unpicked fruit may create a smelly mess on the ground and attract insects and rodents. See Appendix D.

Bauhinia x *blakeana*

Hong Kong Orchid Tree (N)
Fabaceae (Bean Family)

A hybrid originating many years ago in Hong Kong, this species will reach 30 feet in height. Its flowers, a bright rose-purple, are fragrant and appear much of the year. It is sterile and therefore produces no messy beans. It is used in the landscape for its color and light shade, as an accent, or as a screen. It is used as a street tree. Plant it in a light, well-drained soil in full sun. The Hong Kong Orchid Tree grows moderately rapidly. It is heat and wind tolerant and moderately drought tolerant but does not thrive in areas with strong salt winds.

Bauhinia hookeri

Alibangbang (N)
Fabaceae (Bean Family)

Long confused locally with a similar species from the Philippines, this small tree is native to tropical Australia. The Filipino name, Alibangbang, is locally applied to this Aussie relative. A fairly rapid grower, it will reach 25 feet in height and produces a light canopy with pendent branches. Its white flowers appear much of the year and are accented by long reddish stamens that protrude well beyond the petals. Alibangbang is wind tolerant and moderately drought tolerant. It is best away from salt wind. When small it tends to form basal shoots that must be pruned off. This tendency diminishes with maturity. Plant it in full sun in a well-drained soil. It is a fine small tree for residential use and can be used for its shade, for its flowers, or as a screening tree, and it has been successfully used as a street tree.

Bauhinia monandra

H (HPWRA)

Pink Bauhinia, Butterfly Bauhinia (N)
Fabaceae (Bean Family)

Reaching 30 feet in height, this is a moderate grower performing best in an open, well-drained soil in full sun. It is briefly winter deciduous, followed by its showy flowers in late spring. It shows tolerance to wind and heat and moderate tolerance to drought but not to salt. Its plentiful seed pods may be a maintenance problem, but if planted over a shrubby ground cover, they may be absorbed. It is probably native to Southeast Asia. A white flowering variety, *B. monandra* var. *alba*, is also available.

Bauhinia purpurea

H (HPWRA)

Purple Orchid Tree (N)
Fabaceae (Bean Family)

Also from Southeast Asia, this showy tree reaches 30 feet in height, bearing an abundant crop of fragrant flowers that may be pink, red, violet, or white. They are seen mostly in the fall and into winter. A moderate grower, it thrives in a friable, well-drained soil in full sun. It is wind and heat tolerant and moderately drought tolerant but does not show resistance to salt. The Purple Orchid Tree provides a strong color accent in the part of the year when other trees have finished flowering.

Bauhinia tomentosa

Yellow Bauhinia (N) (P)
Fabaceae (Bean Family)

Attaining a height of 20 feet, this tree is native to the wide geographical range from tropical southern and eastern Africa eastward to China. It is drought and wind tolerant but not salt tolerant. Plant it in a hot, full sun area in almost any well-drained soil. It is a moderate grower. It finds good use as a color accent, as its yellow blossoms are seen throughout the year. It can be used as a hedge or screen and has been used as a street tree.

Bolusanthus speciosus

Rhodesian Wisteria Tree (N)
Fabaceae (Bean Family)

This is a beautiful, graceful tree that may grow slowly to 30 feet in height. It is native to hot, dry areas of Angola, South Africa, and north into Mozambique. Flowers borne on pendant racemes are blue-violet, appearing in spring. Foliage is delicate. Plant in full sun in a well-drained soil. It is fairly drought, heat, and wind tolerant. It is a good color and foliar accent. In flower, it forms a strong focal point in the garden. It flowers better at higher, dry elevations but is satisfactory near sea level.

Brexia madagascariensis

Brexia
Grossulariaceae (Gooseberry Family)

From Madagascar, the Seychelles, and East Africa, this handsome small tree grows rather slowly to 30 feet in height, developing a slender, columnar form. Its native habitats are coastal bushland and at the edge of saltwater swamp forests. Its seed is adapted to ocean distribution, retaining viability for several months. It is not particular as to soil, but moisture and good drainage are essential. It is wind and salt-air tolerant. Use Brexia as a vertical accent in a narrow space or grouped to form a windbreak or screening hedge. Its foliage is decorative; flowers are an attractive chartreuse but are inconspicuous.

Brownea latifolia

Mountain Rose (N)
Fabaceae (Bean Family)

Pendent clusters of bright red flowers appear during the winter but also periodically through the year on this small tree from Venezuela and Trinidad and Tobago. Planted in light shade in a rich, well-drained soil with regular watering, the Mountain Rose will grow slowly to 20 feet in height. In its native habitat, it is an understory tree and must have protection from strong wind. New growth is purplish and pendent, turning green upon maturing, providing an interesting focal point. Its bright flowers provide an excellent color accent. It is neither drought nor salt tolerant. Other small Browneas include *B. coccinea* subsp. *coccinea*, the Scarlet Flame Bean; *B. coccinea* subsp. *capitella*, Lantern Brownea; and *Brownea grandiceps*, Rose of Venezuela. All are tropical American, reach 12 feet in height with orange-red flowers, and have the same growth requirements as the Mountain Rose. They are also nitrogen fixers.

Brownea macrophylla

Rouge Puff (N)

Fabaceae (Bean Family)

Panama, Venezuela, and Colombia are home to this 30-foot shrubby tree. (One reference cites a height of 60 feet, but this is far beyond local experience with this species.) It bears large inflorescences of upright, brilliant orange, clustered blooms in winter and spring and periodically throughout the year. It requires moisture and a well-drained soil. Light shade is beneficial, as is protection from wind. A little judicious pruning will help in developing a tree shape. New growth is pendent and purplish-brown, turning green and erect upon maturity. It makes an ideal color accent and garden conversation piece.

Brugmansia x *candida*

Angel's Trumpet, Nānāhonua (P)
Solanaceae (Potato Family)

Growing rapidly to 15 feet in height, this South American tree bears large, pendant, fragrant white flowers through summer and fall. It is a complex hybrid of a number of species. Forms with pale apricot and yellow flowers and variegated foliage are available. Plant it in a moist, well-drained soil in full sun or light shade. It shows moderate tolerance to drought but none to wind and salt. It provides a very strong color accent planted either singly or as a hedge. Flowering is more profuse in cooler elevations. Take extra care to avoid its toxic sap.

Brunfelsia densifolia

Serpentine Hill Raintree (P)
Solanaceae (Potato Family)

Rare and endangered, this Puerto Rican species becomes a slender tree 30 feet in height. Its 5-inch-long tubular flowers are white, turning yellowish with age, and are highly fragrant after dark. Bright orange, spherical fruits add a color accent. A modicum of pruning will assist in enhancing its rather columnar but bushy shape. It requires full sun or light shade, good, rich soil, and ample moisture. It is somewhat wind tolerant but not salt or drought tolerant. Use in the night garden, where its fragrance may be appreciated, and as a shade tree, screen, or hedge. It is a moderately slow grower.

Note: Brunfelsias, like other members of the Potato Family, may contain toxins. It is prudent to avoid ingesting any member of the genus.

Bucida molineti

Dwarf Geometry Tree (T)
Combretaceae (Combretum Family)

Native to the Bahamas, the Dwarf Geometry Tree may reach 25 feet in height, displaying strong horizontal branching. It is a rather slow grower. It thrives in most well-drained soils in sun or light shade. Although partially tolerant of salt air, it should be planted away from extremely salty conditions. It is wind tolerant. Well used as an accent tree for its unusual branching, it is also valued as a tubbed specimen on a sunny lanai or deck.

Callistemon citrinus

Red Bottlebrush, Crimson Bottlebrush
Myrtaceae (Eucalyptus Family)

On its partially pendant branches, bright red flowers clustered into a bottlebrush-shaped inflorescence up to 2 and ¾ inches in length are seen throughout the year on this versatile, evergreen Australian tree. It may reach 30 feet in height. It prefers full sun and a well-drained soil with moderate watering. It is drought and wind tolerant, with moderate tolerance to salt. It develops an excellent canopy, providing light shade, and is useful as a strong color accent, as a screening specimen, or as a windbreak.

Callistemon rigidus

Stiff Bottlebrush
Myrtaceae (Eucalyptus Family)

Another evergreen, somewhat slow growing, small tree from Australia, this species displays a rather rigid form. Branches carry showy red flower spikes, appearing sporadically throughout the year. It has good drought, wind, heat, and salt tolerance. In full sun in any well-drained soil, it will grow to 15 feet in height. It is a good color accent specimen or may be used as a screen or windbreak.

Callistemon viminalis

Weeping Bottlebrush
Myrtaceae (Eucalyptus Family)

A rapid growing, variable species from Queensland, Australia, Weeping Bottlebrush may attain 30 feet in height. Its clustered, bright red, bottlebrush inflorescence may be up to 5 inches in length. They appear on strongly "weeping" branches primarily in spring but may show again lightly throughout the year. Many cultivars have been selected. Some are favored as street trees in its native areas. For best results this species should be planted in a deep, open, moist soil with good drainage and in full sun. It will tolerate light shade and wind. New foliage is soft, fuzzy, and reddish, turning green upon maturity. It is only moderately drought tolerant. Use it for its light shade-producing canopy or as a bright color accent, hedge, or screen.

Cassia roxburghii

Red Cassia (N) (P)
Fabaceae (Bean Family)

Usually flowering in October-November, this colorful species has been known to bloom as early as late August. Red Cassia is native to hot, dry areas of southern India and Sri Lanka. In well-drained soils it grows rather rapidly to 25 feet in height, with a spreading, somewhat drooping evergreen canopy. Red Cassia shows fair tolerance to wind and great tolerance to heat and drought. It is used for its shade and for its unusual, colorful flowering that produces a striking color accent in the garden. Its seed pods are used in veterinary medicine in its native lands.

Cerbera manghas

Sea Mango, Madagascar Ordeal Bean (P) (S)
Apocynaceae (Dogbane Family)

From coastal areas ranging from the Indian Ocean through Southeast Asia, tropical Australia, and the Pacific islands, this tree, readily attaining 30 feet in height, bears white, fragrant flowers much of the year. The seed is poisonous. The tree is salt tolerant, thriving near the high-tide line, and it is wind tolerant but not drought tolerant. Care should be taken when pruning, as the white sap may irritate sensitive skin. In coastal gardens it may be used for its shade, as a tall screen, or as a windbreak. Its large, dark green leaves provide contrast for the small, textured, light gray-green foliage common in beach gardens.

Chrysobalanus icaco

Coco Plum
Chrysobalanaceae (Coco Plum Family)

Reaching 30 feet in height, this native of southern Florida, the West Indies, Mexico, Brazil, and—strangely—tropical West Africa is seen both as a tree and—in dry, salt wind areas—as a shrub to 6 feet. It grows at the edge of both fresh and saltwater swamps, where it becomes a tree, and in dry, onshore salt wind in seaside situations throughout its range, where it develops into a dense 6-foot shrub. It produces an edible "plum" that was an important food for Seminole Indians and is still prized for the jelly made from the fruit. In Mexico parts of the tree are used medicinally and to make a black dye. Its oily seeds are used for food or strung on sticks to make candles. It is heat, salt wind, and drought tolerant and will grow in both poorly drained and well-drained soils and even in pure sand. Use it as a shade tree, windbreak, screen, and for its useful fruit. It is an excellent choice for the beach garden and the xeriscape.

Cinnamomum verum

H (HPWRA)

Ceylon Cinnamon
Lauraceae (Laurel Family)

Originating from the rain forests of Sri Lanka, India, and Burma, this famous tree grows rather slowly to 30 feet in height. An essential oil is derived from young green shoots that provides both strong flavor and a delicate aroma. This is the cinnamon of commerce. Leaves yield another oil that may be used as a substitute for clove. Cinnamon has been prized since ancient times and was an important article of trade with the West. It is mentioned in the Old Testament in the Song of Solomon and the book of Proverbs. Romans favored cinnamon for sacrificial offerings. The tree carries rather dense, evergreen foliage, producing heavy shade. It grows best where some protection from strong winds is available. Plant Ceylon Cinnamon in a rich soil. It requires ample watering. Use it as a shade tree or as a high, screening hedge.

Citrus maxima

Pummelo (T)
Rutaceae (Citrus Family)

A native of Southeast Asia and Malaysia, Pummelo has been cultivated since ancient times. It is a handsome, round-headed evergreen tree reaching 25 feet in height, bearing quantities of large, round, very attractive yellow fruit. A heavy crop may require branch support to prevent breakage. Plant Pummelo in full sun in a rich, well-drained soil and provide regular watering and feeding. It is useful as an ornamental accent in the landscape as well as for its delicious fruit. It is a moderately slow grower. See notes under *Plumeria rubra* below for information concerning the recent introduction of the Papaya Mealybug, which also infests citrus.

Citrus x *reticulata* x *C.* x Tangelo

Tangerine (T)
Rutaceae (Citrus Family)

Among a number of very complex hybrids, two outstanding crosses, 'Fairchild' and 'Page', are grown locally and develop into excellent small trees for the home garden. Citrus growers recommend growing pollinator trees nearby to assure good fruit set. 'Fremont', a Mandarin Orange, is recommended among others to accomplish pollination. When making a selection, be certain that your choice flowers at the same time as the pollinator tree. Tangerine does well in a rich, open, deep soil with good drainage. It is a moderately slow grower, producing a colorful crop of fruit, making it a strong accent in the garden and providing shade. It may be used as a screen or hedge. Other successful citrus, not pictured, include *Citrus nobilis* cv 'Temple' [Temple Orange (T)], which may reach 25 feet in height. It produces best in hot, dry areas, which bring the fruit to full sweetness. It must, however, be watered regularly and planted in a rich, well-drained soil. Pruning will enhance its overall shape. Another citrus, *Citrus reticulata*, Mandarin Orange or Tangerine (T), possibly originating in Southeast Asia and the Philippines, produces a broad canopy reaching 25 feet in height. It is a moderately slow grower. Cultivars 'Dancy' and 'Fremont' are good producers planted in rich, well-watered, well-drained soil. Protection from strong winds is advised. Light pruning will enhance its shape. In addition to its fruit-producing value, this citrus provides a strong color accent and shade. The dense canopies of all citrus make them good screening material.

Clerodendrum quadriloculare
H (HPWRA)

Starburst, Bagauak
Verbenaceae (Verbena Family)

This species from the Philippines will reach 15 feet in height. A little pruning will assist in creating a tree shape. It produces invasive suckers that may be best controlled by planting it within a space surrounded by paving. If planted in a frequently mown grassy area, this may not be a problem. It is spectacular when in bloom during winter and into spring. Its purple under-leaves accent the large flower clusters, as well as providing color throughout the year. Give it a well-drained, rich soil, regular watering, and full sun. It is a great color accent but may also be used for its shade or as a screen or hedge. This Clerodendrum is a moderate grower.

Clusia rosea

Evaluate (HPWRA)

Autograph Tree
Clusiaceae (Clusia Family)

Reaching 30 feet in height, this species, native throughout the Caribbean area, is a tough addition to the landscape. It is drought, wind, and salt tolerant and will grow in almost any garden soil, lava rock, and sand. It is a prime choice for the xeriscape and beach garden and does well in large containers and roof gardens. Its common name comes from the fact that numbers or letters scratched on a leaf will turn white and persist. The inscribed leaves have been used as place cards at a dinner or as a substitute for playing cards. The Autograph Tree is an excellent windbreak, screen, or wide-spreading shade tree. A green-and-white-leaved variegation is available. The seed germinates readily under both dry and moist conditions in soil, on stone walls, or in crotches of trees. It is considered invasive in many areas.

Coffea arabica
H (HPWRA)

Arabian Coffee
Rubiaceae (Coffee Family)

In addition to its importance as a valuable commercial crop, Arabian Coffee is an attractive garden plant. It will grow to 20 feet in height, bearing abundant, highly fragrant white flowers in spring and in the fall a plentiful crop of bright red "berries." It fares best at higher, cooler elevations. Usually grown in full sun, it shows remarkable adaptation to shaded situations and has been used as an indoor tree with strong overhead light. A good, well-drained soil produces good growth. Regular watering and feeding are requirements. Use coffee as a shade tree in narrow spaces or as a screen. Plant it where its fragrance may be enjoyed. It is possibly native to Ethiopia. Arabian Coffee readily naturalizes in moist areas and is best used in drier situations to reduce invasiveness. Another coffee, not shown, is *Coffea liberica*, Liberian Coffee, from tropical West Africa. It is similar in size and may also be developed as an attractive small tree. It does better at lower elevations than Arabian Coffee.

Colobrina oppositifolia

Kauila
Rhamnaceae (Buckthorn Family)

This rare and endangered endemic tree, a slow grower, may eventually reach up to 40 feet in height but is usually a much smaller tree. Found in dry to mesic forest in Oʻahu's Waiʻanae Mountains and on the leeward side of Hawaiʻi, it produces an extremely hard wood formerly used for making spears, *kapa* beaters, and other hard-use articles, in effect taking the place of metal. The wood sinks in water. It is a handsome plant. New growth bears an attractive reddish tomentum. Use Kauila as an accent specimen, providing a point of interest in the landscape. It can also be used as a screen or hedge. It requires a well-drained soil and full sun. It is heat and wind tolerant and shows moderate tolerance to drought.

Cordia lutea

Peruvian Cordia

Boraginaceae (Borage Family)

A small heat-, drought-, and wind-tolerant tree from dry areas of Peru, Ecuador, the Galápagos Islands, and the Marquesas, this species will reach 25 feet in height.

It bears bright yellow flowers throughout the year. It does require minimal pruning to achieve its tree form. Use it as a color accent, a shade tree, or as a screening hedge. Plant it in full sun in a well-drained soil. It is very drought tolerant and will withstand moderate amounts of salt.

Cordia sebestena

Kou Haole, Geiger Tree
Boraginaceae (Borage Family)

Originating from tropical America and the Caribbean Islands, this colorful tree grows slowly to 25 feet in height, displaying clusters of brilliant orange-red flowers much of the year. Its white, fleshy fruits are similarly seen. The tree is best placed away from paved surfaces, where fruitfall may cause slipping. It grows in any well-drained soil and performs best in full sun, although it will also thrive in light shade. Kou Haole has good wind, drought, and salt tolerance and serves well in the landscape as a shade tree, strong color accent, or as a screen.

Crescentia cujete

Calabash Tree
Bignoniaceae (Catalpa Family)

Native to Mexico, northern Central America, and the Caribbean Islands, this tough wind-resistant and rather drought resistant tree will attain 30 feet in height. It has moderate salt tolerance. Flowers, yellowish with purple markings, are borne directly on large branches and the trunk. Its common name relates to its large spherical fruit. It develops a spreading canopy. Plant the Calabash Tree in full sun where it will have space. It is not particular to soil type as long as it is well drained. The dried fruit may be hollowed and used to make containers and musical instruments. Its wood, tough and hard, may be used for making boats and small hard-use articles. With pruning it makes an excellent shade tree. Its corky bark may be used for planting epiphytes such as orchids and bromeliads.

Diphysa americana

Guachipilin, Cuachepil (N)
Fabaceae (Bean Family)

Native to dry parts of tropical Mexico south through Central America, this species will grow moderately slowly to 30 feet in height, although one reference credits it reaching as much as 60 feet in height under optimal conditions. A local mature forty-year-old specimen has grown to only 25 feet in height. Its very fine, almost lacey foliage is contrasted with bright yellow flowers during December and January and sporadically at other times. Plant it in any well-drained soil in full sun. It is quite drought and wind tolerant but is not tolerant of salt. Its bark is attractive, deeply fissured, and suitable for growing small epiphytes. Its wood is hard, heavy, and durable and finds use for wood sculpture, in construction, furniture making, flooring, and general carpentry and is the source of a yellow dye. Use it for its light, shade-producing canopy, which permits the growing of understory plants. Its foliage and strong color provide accents.

Dracaena draco

Dragon Tree
Agavaceae (Agave Family)

A slow-growing tree native to the Canary Islands, Madeira, and the Cape Verde Islands, this species will eventually reach 30 feet or more in height, with a dense, many-branched crown of gray-green leaves. It is quite drought tolerant, wind tolerant, resistant to light salt wind, and thrives in any well-drained soil in full sun. A closely related slow-growing species from the island of Socotra, the Socotran Dragon Tree (*Dracaena cinnaberi*), has similar qualities and garden uses. The bases of old leaves of both are a bright orange color and are prized by arrangers and arts and crafts people. Use both species as strong foliage accents. Both are suitable for the xeriscape.

Dracaena fragrans

Fragrant Dracaena
Agavaceae (Agave Family)

Widely distributed throughout tropical Africa, this small tree may reach 25 feet in height. A good, well-drained soil and regular watering are preferred. The species bears uniformly green foliage. This Dracaena develops a slender canopy, making it ideal for use in narrow spaces. It is good in light shade and, for best foliage production, protected from strong wind. It is its cultivars, however, that have reached great horticultural importance worldwide. These range from cv 'Knerckii', with uniformly light to medium green, drooping leaves, to cv 'Massangeana', with its green, drooping leaves center-striped with yellow and light green. It is popularly known as the Corn Plant. Another cultivar, cv 'Lindenii', bears drooping leaves, green in the center with greenish yellow bands at the sides; cv 'Rothiana' displays narrower, ascending rather than drooping leaves of deep green, strongly banded in white; a rare cultivar, cv 'Victoriae', bears green-centered foliage widely margined in tints of yellow. All forms may be used to create attractive potted or tubbed specimens for interior use, the use most frequently seen in cold and temperate climates. In the tropical landscape, it makes an excellent form and foliage color accent tree and is especially valuable in narrow spaces. It may also be used as a hedge or screen. All produce masses of night-fragrant white flowers.

Dracaena marginata

Madagascar Dragon Tree, Money Tree
Agavaceae (Agave Family)

Slowly forming a broad, round-headed, dense canopy, this tough Madagascan tree attains 25 feet in height. It is wind and drought tolerant and tolerant of salt air. It thrives in almost any well-drained soil. Several cultivars are available, displaying foliage color in pink, white, and green as opposed to the species that has green foliage with mahogany-reddish margins. The Madagascar Dragon Tree has become very popular also as a potted or tubbed specimen and will survive a wide range of interior conditions and abuse. In the garden, use it as a shade tree, an accent against a wall, or use its colorful cultivars as strong color accents. It also may be used as a dense screen, hedge, or windbreak. There is also a very similar but much broader leaved Dracaena available. Its actual identification has not been determined. Plants are derived from cuttings obtained in French Polynesia that were reputedly from Madagascar, but this has not been verified. In any event, it is a useful, strong foliar accent. It is heat, wind, and drought tolerant. Its salt tolerance has not been tested.

D. marginata 'Tricolor'

D. marginata 'Tricolor'

D. marginata 'Colorama'

Eriobotrya japonica
Evaluate (HPWRA)

Loquat
Rosaceae (Rose Family)

A small tree from China and Japan, Loquat may reach 20 feet in height, forming a dense canopy of large, attractive foliage. Its small white flowers are fragrant and are followed by spherical orange fruits in winter. Fruit production is best at cool elevations, although growth is satisfactory at lower elevations. Plant it in full sun in a well-drained, open soil and provide moderate watering. It is wind tolerant and partially drought tolerant. It is a moderately slow grower. In the landscape it provides an ornamental foliage accent or may be used as a screen, as well as a small shade tree.

Erythrina cristi-galli

Common Coral Tree,
Cock's Spur Coral Tree (T) (P) (N)

Fabaceae (Bean Family)

Originating in South America, the Common Coral Tree is a rapid-growing, semideciduous tree reaching 25 feet in height. Flowers varying from deep red to pinkish red appear most of the year but primarily during the winter months. Spent flower stems are persistent and must be cut away to produce satisfactory visual results. It develops a wide crown, requiring space to appear at its best. Almost any well-drained soil, preferably in a sunny spot, will produce good growth and flowering. It requires regular watering. It is a popular color accent and shade tree.

Note: Erythrinas are excellent garden subjects and have been popular for many years. In 2005, however, the Erythrina Gall Wasp (*Quadristichus erythrinae*) found its way to Hawai'i, with devastating results. Until biological controls for this serious pest have been established, the planting of all species of Erythrina is strongly discouraged. The home gardener, using regular spraying with an appropriate insecticide, can, however, control the Erythrina Gall Wasp on *E. cristi-galli*, *E. abyssinica*, and *E. sacleuxii*, all of which show good tolerance to the wasp attacks. Keep other Erythrinas in mind for future planting.

Eugenia brasiliensis

Spanish Cherry, Brazil Cherry
Myrtaceae (Eucalyptus Family)

A small tree from southern Brazil, this species will attain 30 feet in height. It is a slow grower, preferring a rich, well-watered soil. It is wind tolerant but not drought or salt tolerant. Although performing best in full sun, it will tolerate light shade. Dark, lustrous foliage is accented by the red, edible fruit. Use it as a background tree singly or as a screening hedge.

Eugenia uniflora

H (HPWRA)

Surinam Cherry
Myrtaceae (Eucalyptus Family)

Growing rather slowly to 30 feet in height, this Brazilian tree finds many uses in the landscape. Abundant small but attractive white flowers are followed by edible fruit used to make drinks, jams, or jellies. Foliage is pleasantly aromatic, while its bark is decorative. It may be clipped into a tight hedge or used as a screen or windbreak. Best planted in full sun in a friable, well-drained soil, Surinam Cherry responds to regular watering, although moderate drought tolerance is attributed to it. It has no tolerance of salt.

Euphorbia cotinifolia

Red Spurge, Hierba Mala (P) (S)
Euphorbiaceae (Euphorbia Family)

Carrying inconspicuous flowers but very showy reddish foliage, this evergreen tree is native from Mexico to northern South America. It is best grown in full sun in a well-drained soil. It will reach 25 feet in height and is a moderate grower. It has low drought tolerance but no salt or strong wind tolerance. Caution should be exercised in handling this spurge to avoid contact with its sap, which may cause skin irritation. It makes a strong color accent or can be used as a hedge or screen. Light pruning will assist in making it into a small shade tree.

Ficus carica

Common Fig, Fig Tree
Moraceae (Mulberry Family)

A tree reaching 30 feet in height, the fig has been cultivated from ancient times for its edible fruit, eaten either raw or dried, and its shade-producing foliage. From rocky, hot, dry areas of the Middle East, the fig is wind and drought tolerant. Its dense canopy may be broader than the tree's height. It is a moderate grower in almost any well-drained soil. Locally, Chinese prize its fruit for making a delicious soup. We have not found its varietal name. There are, however, a number of named cultivars: 'Excel', a white fig, and 'Kadota', with purple skin, are recommended for local gardens. The fig figures in many myths and legends. It is credited with being man's first clothing, as leaves were strategically placed to hide Adam and Eve's nakedness. Ancient Greeks believed that Bacchus created the fig. Mohammed is quoted as saying, "If I were to say that any fruit had come down from Paradise, I would say it of the Fig." Ancient Egyptians believed that the fig was the favorite food of the Blessed Dead. In addition to its shade-producing canopy and fruit, the fig makes a useful screen or foliar accent. It may be used in the xeriscape.

Ficus dammaropsis

Dinner Plate Fig, Highland Breadfruit
Moraceae (Mulberry Family)

This unusual species is named for its large leaves and fruit, both of which are edible. It is native to the high rainfall areas of upland New Guinea and must be planted in a moist, loamy soil and given ample water. It will thrive in either full sun or light shade. Owing to the size of the leaves, it is best given some protection from strong winds. It will reach 20 feet in height and benefits from a little pruning to give it a better shape. Use it as a shade tree or as a strong foliar accent. The Dinner Plate Fig would be better named the "Turkey Platter Fig," which comes closer to indicating the size of its leaves.

Ficus triangularis

Triangle Leaf Fig
Moraceae (Mulberry Family)

Attaining 20 feet in height, this fig from wet areas of Southeast Asia, Borneo, and the Philippines forms a good small tree. A little judicious pruning will assist in curbing its somewhat sprawling tendency. Plant it in a good, moist, well-drained soil in full sun or light shade. It is wind tolerant but not drought or salt tolerant. It is a useful shade tree in a small space or can be grown to produce a dense screening hedge or windbreak. There is also a green and white variegated form, *F. triangularis* 'Variegata'.

F. triangularis 'Variegata'

Guaiacum officinale

Lignum Vitae
Zygophyllaceae (Tribulus Family)

A slow-growing, bushy tree reaching 25 feet in height, Lignum Vitae is native to Central America and the West Indies. It bears a profusion of bright lavender-blue flowers in late spring and early summer, followed by attractive orange fruits in late summer into winter, providing a good color accent much of the year. While tolerating light shade, it performs best in full sun in a well-drained soil. It is wind and partially drought tolerant but only moderately salt air tolerant. Lignum Vitae wood is extremely hard and is used to make furniture and small hard-use articles. A resin derived from the wood is used medicinally. It is the national tree of Jamaica.

Guaiacum sanctum

Holywood Lignum Vitae
Zygophyllaceae (Tribulus Family)

A closely related species, Holywood Lignum Vitae grows slowly to 20 feet in height and is native to the Florida Keys, larger Caribbean islands, and Central America. It bears its abundant flowers in early spring, but a few may be found into summer. They are a darker, more intense blue than *G. officinale*. Both are good shade and color accent trees, make a good screen or windbreak, and can be used as a tubbed specimen on a hot, windy deck in full sun. Both species display highly attractive bark. It is wind and heat tolerant and is moderately tolerant of drought. Give it a place in the garden in full sun in a well-drained soil.

Guettarda speciosa

Beach Gardenia, Pua Pua, Wut
Rubiaceae (Coffee Family)

Attaining 30 feet or more in height, this coastal species originates from a very wide geographical range extending from the tropical Pacific islands to Australia, Southeast Asia, the Philippines, and islands of the Indian Ocean. Some references attribute a greater height, but local experience indicates a small-tree stature. It is a moderate grower. Its small white flowers are fragrant, especially at night, and are seen throughout the year. In India the flowers are thought to promote relaxation. In Micronesia they may be made into garlands, worn in the hair, or used for scenting coconut oil. It is the flower emblem of the Marshall Islands. Bark, leaves, and fruit have medicinal uses. The durable wood is used for light construction; in Tonga, tapa anvils are made from this tree. In Kiribati and Tuvalu, it figures in myths and legends. Growing best in a sandy soil, it will also thrive in a well-drained loam. It is salt tolerant but does better with protection from wind, which damages its large leaves. An excellent choice for the beach garden. A good shade tree and foliage accent among small-leaved, dark green plants.

Haematoxylon campechianum

Logwood (N)
Fabaceae (Bean Family)

A small, slow-growing tree reaching 30 feet in height, this species is from tropical America. Although in its native areas it is frequently found in semimarshland, it has naturalized in rather dry places in Hawai'i. Plant it in a well-drained, open soil in full sun. Its dark red heartwood is used to make furniture, dyes, and stains. It has medicinal uses. Use it for its dense, shade-producing canopy or as a screen or windbreak. Its small racemes of creamy white flowers are fragrant.

Harpephyllum caffrum

Kaffir Plum (s)
Anacardiaceae (Cashew Family)

This slow-growing South African tree will reach 30 feet in height. It must have full sun and a well-drained soil. It is wind and heat tolerant and moderately drought toler-ant. It bears small, sour fruits highly prized for making a delicious jelly. The fruit and all parts of the tree should be handled with caution to avoid contact with its sap, which, like almost all members of the Cashew Family, contains substances that may result in skin eruptions on persons who are susceptible. It is a good shade tree and can be used as a windbreak.

Harpullia pendula
Tulipwood Tree
Sapindaceae (Soapberry Family)

From Australia, the Tulipwood Tree will reach 25 feet in height, bearing insignificant flowers, followed by highly attractive fruit. Its dense crown of evergreen foliage makes it an excellent shade tree for small spaces, as well as a screening tree. It thrives in sun or part shade in most well-drained soils. Its wood is used by furniture and cabinetmakers.

Hibiscus arnottianus subsp. *punaluuensis*

Kokiʻo Keʻokeʻo, Punaluʻu White Hibiscus
Malvaceae (Hibiscus Family)

Native to the Koʻolau Range on Oʻahu, this excellent endemic tree will grow to 30 feet in height. It is a moderately rapid grower. It bears masses of white, fragrant flowers most of the year. They may be used to make leis. It is fairly wind tolerant and partially salt-air tolerant but requires regular watering to produce heavy foliage and bloom. A rich, moist, well-drained soil will bring top results. Use the Punaluʻu White Hibiscus as a good shade tree, a hedge or screen, or as a floral focus. Pruning will assist in producing the traditional tree shape.

Hibiscus clayi

Clay's Kokiʻo
Malvaceae (Hibiscus Family)

Occurring in fairly low, somewhat dry elevations in eastern Kauaʻi, this highly ornamental endemic will grow slowly to 20 feet in height. It bears a profusion of dark red flowers. Horticultural requirements are the same as for Kokiʻo ʻUla, but it will tolerate short periods of drought. The flowers are used by the lei maker. It makes a fine color accent or can be used to form a hedge or background for other smaller species. A bit of judicious pruning will enhance the overall attractiveness.

Hibiscus hamabo

Hamabo
Malvaceae (Hibiscus Family)

Producing a rounded, dense, evergreen canopy of dark green foliage, this tree from southern Japan and the Bonin Islands will reach 30 feet in height and is a moderately rapid grower. It bears large yellow flowers most of the year. Plant it in full sun in a good, well-drained soil and provide regular watering. It is moderately wind and salt tolerant. Use it as a fine shade tree or as a tall windbreak, screen, or hedge.

Hibiscus kokio

Koki'o 'Ula
Malvaceae (Hibiscus Family)

A beautiful endemic rather slowly reaching 20 feet in height, Koki'o 'Ula bears bright red, orange-red, orange, or, not commonly, yellow flowers. They may be used by the lei maker. It is found on all the major islands except Ni'ihau and Kaho'olawe in partially dry to wet forests. It thrives in a rich, well-drained soil and grows more strongly in full sun, but it will produce satisfactorily in light shade. Pruning is required to produce a good tree shape. Use it as a good color accent or focal point. It can be espaliered easily.

Hibiscus waimeae

Koki'o Ke'oke'o, Koki'o Kea
Malvaceae (Hibiscus Family)

This small endemic tree is found from upper Waimea Canyon to the western and northern coasts of Kaua'i. It will reach 30 feet in height, bearing large, white, fragrant flowers that may be used by the lei maker. It is a moderate grower. Although growing best in good, well-drained, moist soils, it also occurs at lower, drier elevations of Waimea Canyon. Once established it may tolerate some drought. It has fair wind tolerance. It may be trained into a good shade tree or may be used as a screening hedge and floral accent.

Ipomoea pauciflora

Tree Morning Glory, Casahuate, Palo del Muerto (P)
Convolvulaceae (Morning Glory Family)

A highly ornamental tree from arid parts of tropical Mexico and Central America, the Tree Morning Glory produces clusters of large white flowers along its arching branches during late fall and winter months when it is partially leafless. Its bark is white. It is drought, heat, and wind tolerant. It may grow to 25 feet in height. The seeds, which are not produced locally, are poisonous and contain hallucinogenic substances. There are, however, several medicinal uses, including the treatment of rattlesnake bite and the treatment of paralysis. The Spanish name, Palo del Muerto, translates as "Walking Stick of the Dead," no doubt in reference to its poisonous character. It makes a striking floral accent during months when other trees are not flowering.

Jatropha integerrima

Rose-Flowered Jatropha, Peregrina (P)+ (S)+
Euphorbiaceae (Euphorbia Family)

This bushy evergreen tree will reach 20 feet in height. It is native to the West Indies and produces its red flowers throughout the year. Plant it in full sun in a well-drained soil. As it is a member of the Euphorbia Family, take care to avoid its sap when pruning or handling. It is partially wind tolerant but is not drought or salt tolerant. It makes a color accent and can be used en masse as a colorful hedge or screen. A little pruning will hasten its tree shape. There is also a pink-flowered form. See notes under *Plumeria rubra* for information relative to the new Papaya Mealybug, which infests Jatrophas.

Kokia drynarioides

Kokiʻo, Hau Hele ʻUla
Malvaceae (Hibiscus Family)

An endangered endemic, this species will reach 25 feet in height. It is a tree for dry areas above 1,000 feet but also thrives at lower levels and produces flowers. It carries large ornamental leaves and beautiful, large, bright red blossoms. It was formerly cultivated by Hawaiians for its flowers and for its bark, which yields a dye. It is easily cultivated in very open, well-drained soils. Use it as a brilliant color accent planted in full sun in a very well-drained soil. Once established, water sparingly.

Kopsia arborea

Penang Sloe (P)
Apocynaceae (Dogbane Family)

Originating in high rainfall areas of Java and Australia, this species will grow rather slowly to 20 feet in height. It thrives in a rich, well-drained soil. Flowers, borne abundantly, are white and fragrant and may be seen sporadically throughout the year. Its purplish fruit contains a toxic substance. A rain forest tree, this species requires regular watering. It has no drought and little wind tolerance. It makes an excellent accent tree. Plant it where the fragrance of its flowers may be experienced. Old leaves turn red and are attractive.

Kopsia pruniformis

Java Prune (P)
Apocynaceae (Dogbane Family)

A small forest tree from Java, *Kopsia pruniformis* will slowly reach 30 feet in height. During most of the year, it bears clusters of fragrant white flowers followed by attractive purplish fruit. The fruit contains a toxic substance. Avoid them. Plant this species in a rich, moist, well-drained soil. It is partially wind resistant but has no tolerance of drought or salt. Use it as an accent, a screening tree, or a tall hedge. Its lustrous dark green foliage would make a good accent against a dark wall or light green foliage. Old leaves turn bright red. A close relative, not pictured, is *Kopsia fruticosa*, Pink Kopsia from India to Thailand, Indonesia, and the Philippines. It reaches 20 feet in height and requires the same growing conditions as the Java Prune. It also bears toxic fruit and, obviously, pink, fragrant flowers.

Lagerstroemia archeriana

Australian Queen Flower
Lythraceae (Crape Myrtle Family)

Native to moist areas of north Queensland and Western Australia as well as Timor and New Guinea, this delicate evergreen tree slowly reaches 30 feet in height. It is a welcome color accent in late spring and early summer.

Flowers, a light pinkish-mauve, are borne abundantly. The bark is decorative, showing white, tan, and light brown. Dried seed pods are used by wreath makers and flower arrangers. Its overall form tends to be more columnar than spreading, providing a candidate for narrow spaces or a dooryard specimen and for screening. It is wind but not drought or salt tolerant. Give it good, well-drained soil with regular watering.

Lagerstroemia indica

Crape Myrtle
Lythraceae (Crape Myrtle Family)

A small tree from China growing to 30 feet in height, Crape Myrtle bears masses of colorful flowers in summer. It is a moderate grower. Its plentiful flowers range from pink to white to lavender-purple, with many named cultivars. Its smooth bark is ornamental, showing patches of tan and gray. It is wind resistant and will tolerate some drought once well established. Plant it in full sun in a rich, well-drained soil. Water deeply but not often. It makes a good shade tree but finds its highest use as a strong color accent. It also finds use as a screen or hedge.

Lawsonia inermis

Henna
Lythraceae (Crape Myrtle Family)

Native from North Africa to southern Asia, this is the source of the popular reddish-orange dye, henna, used in ancient times by the Egyptians and, later, by westerners and Mohammedans. Crushed leaves mixed with an acid produce the famous dye. It reaches 20 feet in height, bearing fragrant flowers of white or red. Once established, it is very drought tolerant and withstands heat and wind. It is rather slow growing. A bit of pruning will hasten the production of a tree form.

Ligustrum sinense

H (HPWRA)

Chinese Privet
Oleaceae (Olive Family)

Native to southern China, this privet will reach 20 feet in height. It bears small, dark green leaves and has for many years been prized for clipping into hedges or topiary and carefully shaped in local Japanese gardens. Pruning is required to develop a tree form. It thrives best in a good, well-drained soil in either full sun or light shade. It is wind tolerant and moderately drought tolerant but shows little tolerance of salt air. Under ideal conditions, it may be a rapid grower. There is a green-and-white-leaved variegated form that tends to be shorter and bushier than the species. It is useful in providing a bright spot in the landscape and, with night lighting, it is quite dramatic.

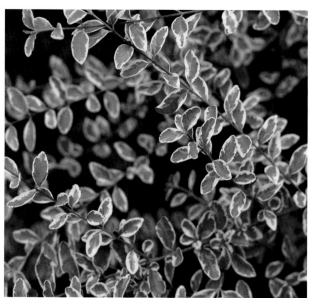

Lysiloma bahamensis

Wild Tamarind, Caribbean Walnut (N) (P)
Fabaceae (Bean Family)

A small evergreen tree from the Bahamas, Florida, the West Indies, and Mexico, this species will attain 30 feet or a bit more in height. It bears small but attractive white powder-puff blossoms. Foliage is very fine, its wide-spreading, weeping canopy casting a light shade, permitting the growth of grass below. It is wind, salt, heat, and drought tolerant. It grows in a wide range of soils, as long as they are well drained. This is an excellent choice for a coastal garden exposed to salt wind and is a good selection for the xeriscape. Use it for its shade or as a textural accent among species with large dark green foliage. Its hard wood is used for flooring and cabinetry, as one of its common names suggests.

Lysiphyllum cunninghamii

Kimberley Bauhinia, Bohenia Tree (N) (P)
Fabaceae (Bean Family)

Growing rather slowly to 30 feet in height, this small tree from dry parts of northern Australia is highly drought, heat, and wind tolerant. It will thrive in most well-drained soils. Flowers displaying pink petals with protruding red stamens are borne on its pendulous branches. Leaves vary from blue-grey to grey-green. The bark, used in Aboriginal medicine as an antiseptic wash, contains an antibacterial constituent. A thick exudate of the bark, known as "toffee," is edible. A modern essence extracted from the tree reputedly encourages open-mindedness and the ability to embrace new concepts. Its slender canopy produces a light shade. It forms a good foliar and flower accent specimen. It is a candidate for the xeriscape.

Majidia zanquebarica

Zanzibar Soapberry, Velvet Seed
Sapindaceae (Soapberry Family)

A highly variable species from East Africa and Madagascar, the Zanzibar Soapberry is described as ranging in size from a shrub to a timber tree. Its geographical range places it in both dry and heavy rainfall areas, which is doubtless responsible for the development of variations. Locally, the Zanzibar Soapberry grows rather rapidly into a small tree reaching 30 feet in height. It produces a rounded canopy, providing light shade. Its main attraction is the crop of seed pods following its insignificant flowers. The pods, about an inch across, open to display a bright red interior with dark, purplish-blue, fuzzy seeds; both the interior and the seeds retain their color when dry. These are highly prized by lei makers and flower arrangers. Plant the Zanzibar Soapberry in a well-drained soil in full sun and use it as a good shade tree or an accent where its showy pods may be appreciated.

Malpighia emarginata

Acerola, Barbados Cherry
Malpighiaceae (Malpighia Family)

Native to tropical Central America, this useful small tree grows to 20 feet in height. Attractive pink to purple flowers are followed by bright red, tart fruits prized for their high Vitamin C content. Up to three crops a year may be realized if regularly watered. Superior cultivars have been selected, which include 'Manoa Sweet', bearing a nontart fruit, and 'B-15', with improved fruit and crop size. Acerola performs best in a hot, dry area in full sun and planted in a well-drained, open soil. It shows moderate drought, heat, and wind tolerance but not good salt tolerance. In addition to its edible fruit use, it can be shaped into a small shade tree or as a screen, windbreak, or hedge. As with other fruit trees, plant it where its fruit may be readily harvested or over a ground cover that raking will not disturb.

Mangifera indica

Mango dwarf varieties (s)
Anacardiaceae (Cashew Family)

Horticulturists have developed dwarf varieties of this normally large tree. Considerable work is ongoing, especially in India, to increase the numbers of such varieties and the quality of fruit. 'Julie', a variety developed in Trinidad and Tobago, grows to 20 feet in height. It fruits best in hot, dry areas. 'Fairchild' also reaches 20 feet in height and produces well in areas with a more moderate climate. It bears a crop of sweet, fiberless fruit. Both varieties produce a dense, compact canopy that is wind and moderately drought tolerant. Use the dwarfs as a hedge or screen or as an accent tree. They are relatively slow growers. Plant them where the fruit may be easily picked, using caution to avoid skin contact with their sap, which may cause skin irritation. In addition to fruit, these dwarfs provide tough foliage for making fine screening hedges or windbreaks.

Manilkara zapota

Chicle Tree, Sapodilla
Sapotaceae (Sapodilla Family)

From its original habitats in Central America, the Chicle Tree or Sapodilla was spread throughout the American tropics in pre-Columbian times and today is also grown throughout tropical Asia. The tree carries a dense canopy of dark green, leathery leaves, producing an attractive accent in the landscape, or it may be used as a screen and as a source of excellent fruit. It will thrive in almost any soil, even sand, as long as it has good drainage. Once established it is fairly wind, heat, and drought tolerant and shows good tolerance of salt. The Chicle Tree is quite slow growing and will eventually exceed our 30-foot ceiling. Improved cultivars, which may not exceed the "small tree" definition, include 'Martin', with large, round fruit containing white pulp, and 'Makok', which has a high fruit production and bears small, highly sweet fruit with orange pulp. Others, not pictured, include 'Gonzales', 'Tikal', 'Alano', and 'Ponderosa', all highly recommended for the small residential garden.

Melaleuca bracteata
'Revolution Gold'

Black Tea Tree, 'Revolution Gold'
Myrtaceae (Eucalyptus Family)

A rather recent sport of a common Melaleuca native to Australia, 'Revolution Gold' has become an extremely popular small tree there, prized for its bright yellow foliage. A moderately rapid grower, this tree will reach 25 feet in height, developing a dense canopy. It is a strong color accent in the garden or may be used as a windbreak or screen. It is wind tolerant, partially drought tolerant, but only moderately salt tolerant. Plant it in full sun in an open, well-drained soil.

Metrosideros polymorpha

Lehua, 'Ōhi'a Lehua
Myrtaceae (Eucalyptus Family)

Although under perfect conditions in the wild this endemic species may reach 100 feet in height, it is also encountered as a shrub. It is of such slow growth that it can be recommended for use as a small, columnar tree. Some pruning may be necessary. It is a highly variable tree: leaf size, shape, and texture may vary from one population to the next, while newly opened colored leaves (*liko*) vary from translucent red to opaque orange, lavender, or white, and leaf bud (*mu'o*) color variations are frequently encountered. It is the blossom, however, that attracts maximum attention. Color ranges from white (rare) through pale yellow, strong yellow, orange, and gold to reds and dark red. Leis are commonly made from the flower as well as from the *liko* and *mu'o*. The rich red-flowered lei was prized by the Volcano Goddess Pele. While a rich, moist soil will produce better growth and bloom, 'Ōh'ia Lehua will thrive in almost any soil as long as drainage is excellent. It does not tolerate soggy, poorly aerated soils. In the wild it is found on bare lava as well as good forest loam. This valuable ornamental is wind tolerant and partially salt-air tolerant and, in the wild, may even be found in extremely hot, dry locations. Nurseries specializing in native Hawaiian plants carry rather large, tubbed specimens whose flower color, *liko*, and foliage can be seen and evaluated for the gardener's selection. Hawaiians traditionally used its hard, tough wood for carving religious images and for fashioning spears, mallets, and other hard-use articles. Today the wood is prized for furniture making and flooring.

Metrosideros tremuloides

Lehua ʻĀhihi
Myrtaceae (Eucalyptus Family)

A slow-growing, small endemic tree found only on
Oʻahu, Lehua ʻĀhihi will reach 15 feet in height, with a
somewhat weeping habit. Its red flowers are used by the
lei maker. The first verse of Queen Liliʻuokalani's well-
known "Aloha ʻOe," composed in Maunawili in 1877,
refers to "seeking the buds and miniature lehua flowers
of the uplands." This is a good small tree for moist areas.
A rich, well-drained soil produces the best results. It is
wind tolerant. It makes a fine color accent, as well as providing lei-making flowers and a landscape conversation
piece.

Moringa oleifera

Horseradish Tree, Ben Oil Tree, Kalamungay
Moringaceae (Drumstick Tree Family)

Now widely planted throughout the tropics, the Horseradish Tree is native to dry areas of India, Arabia, and possibly to Africa and the East Indies. All parts of the tree furnish useful products: grated roots provide a strong substitute for horseradish, and young foliage is eaten as greens, in salads, vegetable curries, and for seasoning. In Malaysia, seeds are eaten much as westerners eat peanuts. Seeds yield a fine, nondrying oil, called ben oil, which is used to lubricate watches and fine machinery. There are many medicinal properties. In Africa its branches are used as a charm against witchcraft. The Horseradish Tree grows rapidly to 30 feet in height, presenting a slender form with drooping branches. Provide a well-drained soil in a partially dry place in full sun. When harvesting edible parts, seeds, and young shoots, cut carefully to retain the shape of the tree. Unharvested pods are light brown and quite persistent. They eventually drop and can be a source of litter. It produces its clusters of small white flowers throughout the year. Use it not only for its edible qualities but for a source of light shade or a small textured accent where its delicate foliage may be appreciated. It is more a tree for the edible garden than a subject for general landscaping. Locally, the Horseradish Tree is highly prized by Filipinos.

Munroidendron racemosum

Munroidendron
Araliaceae (Panax Family)

An endemic tree reaching 25 feet in height, Munroidendron is native to Kaua'i. It is endangered but readily grown under cultivation. It is a fairly rapid grower. It is moderately wind, drought, and salt tolerant. Use it as an accent or specimen plant against dark green, fine-textured material. Its ornamental foliage and unusual inflorescence form a good vertical accent in the landscape. Plant it in full sun in a good, well-drained soil. Water moderately.

Myoporum sandwicense

Naio, Bastard Sandalwood
Myoporaceae (Myoporum Family)

This is a good selection for difficult garden situations: Naio is heat, drought, salt, and wind tolerant. Its thick canopy crowns a tree up to 30 feet in height. It grows well, although somewhat slowly, in almost any soil as long as it has good drainage. Some pruning may be desirable to hasten a good tree shape. Naio is native to both dry and moist places in the Hawaiian Islands. It is valued as a windbreak, screen, or, given time, for its light shade. Its wood is fragrant, somewhat like that of Sandalwood, and was at one time substituted for it. Hawaiians traditionally used Naio's tough wood in house building. Variable in leaf size and shape, there is also a decumbent form used as a ground cover.

Napoleonaea imperialis

Napoleon's Buttons
Lethycidaceae (Brazil Nut Family)

A small, slender tree from tropical West Africa, this species is grown for its strange flowers—looking much like fancy buttons—that appear on the trunk. It will grow slowly to 20 feet in height in both full sun and light shade. Provide a rich, well-watered soil and some protection from strong wind. It has no tolerance to salt. It is a good choice for a narrow garden space or to frame a doorway planted where the "buttons" may be seen.

Nolina recurvata

Pony Tail, Beaucarnea
Agavaceae (Agave Family)

In full sun and planted in a well-drained soil, this unusual tree will grow rather slowly to 30 feet in height. It branches widely and develops a broad, water-storing base. Give it plenty of room. The deserts of northern Mexico are the home of this tree. It is highly drought and wind tolerant and tolerates moderate salt-air exposure. It is an excellent accent specimen or may be clustered to form an unusual grove. Old, multibranched specimens produce excellent shade. It is good in the xeriscape.

Ochna integerrima

Tet Tree
Ochnaceae (Mickey Mouse Plant Family)

Growing slowly to 30 feet in height, the Tet Tree is native to the wide area of tropical Asia from northeast India to the Malay Peninsula, Thailand, Vietnam, and Hainan Island. In Vietnam it bears bright yellow blossoms during the Lunar New Year, when Vietnamese observe holiday celebrations known as Tet. In Hawai'i it flowers sparingly several times during the year, with the heaviest flowering in June. In its native areas it is found in both moist and dry deciduous forest. Plant it in a rich, well-drained soil. It is somewhat wind tolerant but shows no tolerance to salt. It makes a good color accent and can be made into a shade tree, screen, or hedge. Its cultural association makes it a good garden conversation piece.

Ochrosia elliptica
New Caledonia Tree, Pokosola (P)
Apocynaceae (Dogbane Family)

A small tree slowly reaching 25 feet in height, Pokosola originates from tropical Australia and New Caledonia. Dark green foliage is accented by bright red fruit. The tree likes a rich, well-drained, moist soil and will grow in full sun or light shade in both coastal and inland gardens. In Hawaiʻi, the seeds are made into jewelry. It may be used as an accent specimen, a hedge, or a windbreak. Some references allude to the presence of toxic sap. Use caution in handling.

Pandanus tectorius

Hala, Screwpine (T)
Pandanaceae (Screwpine Family)

Found on many tropical islands throughout the Pacific Ocean, hala, a native species, grows to 30 feet in height, with a broadly spreading crown usually supported by a system of aerial roots. It is a moderate grower. It is highly wind and salt tolerant and is an excellent small tree for a beachside garden. It thrives in almost any well-drained soil, even pure beach sand in full sun, but it will tolerate light shade. Its fruit ranges from orange to orange-red to red and is used to make long-lasting leis. Its fragrant, white male blossoms are similarly used. Leaves, an attractive bluish-green, are used to fashion mats and a wide variety of containers. Fallen leaves must be raked up regularly. Use gloves; their spiny edges can inflict a painful scratch. There are, however, cultivars that are spineless, as well as several with green and yellow striping. *P. tectorius* var. *laevis*, called Lau Hala Kilipaki in Hawaiian, is grown for its spineless leaves that can be fashioned into plaited products. *Pandanus tectorius* cv 'Baptistii' is prized for its highly ornamental, spineless leaves whose midrib is strongly striped in yellow. It is used by the flower arranger as well as in the landscape as a color accent. It is especially dominant in the garden when lighted at night. Another hala, *P. tectorius* cv 'Veitchii', bears foliage with white stripes near the leaf margin. Spines are greatly reduced. It is similarly valued as a color accent and in the lighted night garden.

P. tectorius var. *baptistii*

P. tectorius var. *baptistii*

P. tectorius var. *laevis*

P. tectorius var. *veitchii*

Parmentiera aculeata

Cuajilote, Guachilote (т)

Bignoniaceae (Catalpa Family)

A small tree from tropical Mexico and south to Guatemala, Cuajilote grows rather slowly to 30 feet or slightly more in height. It bears flowers of green and mauve directly on the trunk and large branches. These are followed by sweet, yellow fruit, eaten both raw and cooked. Plant it in full sun in a well-drained soil. It tolerates heat, wind, and moderate drought. Its rough bark makes a good home for small epiphytes. While pruning or harvesting, avoid the small spines found at leaf bases. Use it as an accent tree or another conversation piece.

Parmentiera cerifera

Candle Tree
Bignoniaceae (Catalpa Family)

Growing to 30 feet in height, this tree from Panama and tropical Mexico is a good choice for a small tree in the landscape. The whitish flowers are borne throughout the year on the trunk and main branches, producing foot-long, slender fruits hanging like candles. This character is the source of its common name. The fruit may be stewed and used in salads; it also has medicinal uses. Planted in full sun, it prefers a well-drained, moist soil. It is wind tolerant but does not thrive under drought conditions. With minor pruning, it makes an interesting shade tree.

Phyllanthus acidus

Otaheite Gooseberry
Euphorbiaceae (Euphorbia Family)

Grown for its large crop of small, yellow, round, acid fruits, this tree, possibly originating in Madagascar, will reach 30 feet in height. Flowers are reddish but not outstanding. It is a moderate grower. Any friable, well-drained soil with regular but not heavy watering will produce optimal growth. It thrives best in full sun. The fruit is used in cooking. In India it has medicinal uses. In addition to its edible fruit, use it for its light shade or as a textural accent, where its small-leaved canopy may be a foil for other species with large-leaved, dark green foliage.

Pisonia grandis cv 'Alba'

Moonlight Tree, Lettuce Tree
Nyctaginaceae (Four-O'Clock Family)

This small evergreen tree from Malaysia attains 20 feet in height. It is grown for its large, highly ornamental semisucculent leaves, which are a pleasing chartreuse. It requires a good, well-drained soil, regular watering, and protection from strong wind. It shows moderate salt and drought tolerance and performs best when not subjected to drying. It is a moderate grower. Plant the Moonlight Tree as a bright accent among darker, small-textured plants or against a dark stone wall. It is beautiful at night with up-lighting.

Pittosporum confertiflorum

Hō‘awa
Pittosporaceae (Pittosporum Family)

An endemic Hawaiian species reaching 25 feet in height, this species will grow at low elevations. In the wild it is found in both dry and wet forests in full sun and light shade. Good drainage and moderate watering are essential to good growth and flowering. Flowers are white to cream colored and are fragrant at night. It is a good small shade tree and can be used as a screen. Plant it where its flowers may be appreciated. It is somewhat slow growing and fairly wind tolerant but not salt tolerant. See also *P. flocculosum* and *P. hosmeri*. All have important botanical differences but minor differences insofar as landscape use is concerned. They may vary according to their response to one's garden environment.

Pittosporum flocculosum

Hōʻawa
Pittosporaceae (Pittosporum Family)

This rare, small endemic tree from Oʻahu is found at fairly low elevations in both wet and semidry places and grows readily in a garden setting given good drainage, full sun, and regular watering. It is a moderate grower, attaining up to 30 feet in height. Flowers are white, turning cream colored, and are fragrant after dark. It provides a small spot of shade and makes a good screen or windbreak. Place it where its fragrance may be appreciated in the evening. It is quite wind tolerant and semidrought tolerant but not salt tolerant.

Pittosporum hosmeri

Hōʻawa
Pittosporaceae (Pittosporum Family)

This endemic species will reach 30 feet in height, bearing a dense canopy of leaves. Flowers are white and highly fragrant at night. Position it in full sun or light shade. It is a moderate grower, thriving in almost any well-drained soil. This species will tolerate light wind but has no salt-air or drought tolerance. Hawaiians used parts of the fruit medicinally. Plant it where its fragrance may be enjoyed. It makes a slender shade tree or hedge or screen planting.

Pittosporum viridiflorum
Evaluate (HPWRA)

Cape Pittosporum
Pittosporaceae (Pittosporum Family)

A small, tough tree reaching 25 feet in height, Cape Pittosporum is wind and partially drought tolerant. It is native to parts of South Africa, Madagascar, and southern India and displays wide variability in growth. It develops a heavy canopy of dark green leaves and bears fragrant flowers. A slow grower, it will thrive in any well-drained soil with moderate watering. It makes a good screen or windbreak. It grows best in cool areas.

Platycladus orientalis

Oriental Arbor Vitae

Cupressaceae (Cypress Family)

China and Korea are the homes of this evergreen tree, which is variable as to size, foliage color, and shape. The form widely planted in Hawai‘i grows somewhat slowly to 30 feet in height. It is wind tolerant and, if given minimal protection, will grow in coastal gardens. Give it a loamy soil with good drainage in full sun. It may be used as windbreak, screen, or as an accent, where its unusual conical form is the focus of the landscape. Old specimens may be trained with pruning into producing a small shade tree.

Pleomele hawaiiensis

Hala Pepe

Agavaceae (Agave Family)

There are six endemic species of Hala Pepe, all of them highly attractive and bearing beautiful greenish-yellow flowers in dense, pendant inflorescences. All are called Hala Pepe. *Pleomele hawaiiensis*, once plentiful, is now rare and endangered. It is a slow grower, eventually reaching 20 feet in height with several branches. Its abundant flowers, prized by the lei maker, are borne on a pendent stalk. It is sacred to Laka, goddess of hula, and was one of the plants placed on her hula altar. It is still found in dry areas of Kona at elevations from 1,500 to 2,400 feet elevation, although it will grow successfully at lower elevations. Drainage is critical. Plant this species in full sun in an open soil, even ʻaʻā, and water sparingly. It is heat, wind, and somewhat drought tolerant. *Pleomele aurea* (not pictured) occurs on Kauaʻi in somewhat dry areas from near sea level to moist areas at a 3,000-foot elevation. It grows slowly into a tree reaching 30 feet in height. Plant *P. aurea* in full sun in a rich, moist soil. Good drainage is essential. It is wind tolerant and moderately drought tolerant.

Plumeria lambertiana

Baja Plumeria (P) (S)
Apocynaceae (Dogbane Family)

An extremely drought and heat tolerant species from the southern tip of Baja California, this plumeria was collected growing among arborescent cacti and thorn scrub. It is a valuable tree, reaching 20 feet in height with a columnar habit of growth. It is moderately slow growing. Its white, fragrant flowers are borne abundantly. It provides a strong flowering accent but not much shade due to its growth habit. It is a good candidate for the xeriscape. Plant it in full sun in a well-drained soil and water sparingly once established. Planted on both sides of a walkway exposed to hot sun, it will provide welcome shade in a constricted space.

Note: For all plumeria, see notes below under *Plumeria rubra* for information relative to the Papaya Mealybug, which may infest your plumerias.

Plumeria obtusa

Singapore Plumeria (P) (S) and Bahama Plumeria
Apocynaceae (Dogbane Family)

Native to the West Indies, the Singapore Plumeria grows to a little over 30 feet in height. It is semideciduous, dropping much of its large, shiny green canopy during the winter months and coming into massive bloom in early spring. Flowering continues into fall. The large, white, fragrant flowers are used in arrangements but not usually made into leis due to their oversize, rather floppy nature, and short-lived attractiveness. A well-drained soil in full sun produces best results. It is a moderate grower. Regular irrigation, in spite of its partially arid native home, provides high flower production. It is an excellent floral accent and overall shade tree. It serves well as a screen or windbreak. Dwarf forms are also available.

A form of *Plumeria obtusa* was introduced to local gardens a number of years ago from the Bahamas. Taxonomically it is *Plumeria obtusa*, but for the sake of gardeners we are taking the liberty of calling it "Bahama Plumeria." It is significantly different as far as the landscaper is concerned. It will reach 25 feet in height, bearing rough leaves about a quarter of the size of the common Singapore Plumeria, abundant but smaller fragrant flowers, and, with nearly vertical growth, it develops a narrow canopy. It is native to coastal areas of the Bahamas and is salt, wind, and drought tolerant. It does not drop its leaves during the winter months. It is a good candidate for the xeriscape and beach garden. Water sparingly once established. Full sun is a must.

P. obtusa 'Bahama'

P. obtusa 'Bahama'

Plumeria obtusa var. *sericifolia*

Dominican Plumeria (P) (S)
Apocynaceae (Dogbane Family)

A highly useful species from hot, dry, coastal areas of the Dominican Republic, this plumeria is characterized by its rather husky growth and the pyramidal but not sharp lumps that develop on older branches. It reaches 30 feet in height, with an equal spread. It is heat, wind, drought, and moderately salt tolerant, a good candidate for both xeriscape and the coastal garden. Its 2-inch, fragrant white flowers are borne abundantly during spring and summer. It does not lose its leaves in winter. In addition to its shade-giving qualities, it may be used as a wind-break or screen. Plant it in full sun in a well-drained soil. Water sparingly once established.

Plumeria pudica

Puerto Rican Frangipani (s)
Apocynaceae (Dogbane Family)

An evergreen tree from the West Indies and Venezuela, this plumeria grows to 20 feet in height. It bears unusual foliage described as "spoon shaped" or lobed. The canopy, which is somewhat columnar, tends to become quite dense. Some pruning is recommended to thin the canopy as protection against strong winds, or plant it in a protected place. It likes full sun and good drainage. It has moderate salt tolerance and good drought tolerance once established. Its unscented white flowers are borne abundantly during the warm months. It is useful as a flowering accent, a background for smaller species, or it may be planted as a screen or as a shade tree in a narrow space.

Plumeria rubra (hybrids)

Plumeria, Temple Tree (P) (S)
Apocynaceae (Dogbane Family)

Although slightly exceeding our height limitation for small trees, *Plumeria rubra* is such a popular ornamental tree that it is included here. It is commonly seen locally used as a small tree. Originating in semidry parts of tropical Mexico, this tree prefers a sunny location in a well-drained soil. It is a moderate grower and is deciduous during the winter months. Following the leafless period, large clusters of prized, fragrant flowers are produced. Flowering continues for six months. It develops a broad canopy and must be given space. Over a hundred cultivars have been selected from seedlings, providing a range of flower color from white to yellow, gold, orange, light pink to dark pink, light red to dark red, and bicolors. There are also large flowers, small flowers, and even a semidouble flowered form. Several dwarf growing selections are also available. Pictured are several cultivars displaying the range of flower colors commonly seen. Although derived from areas considered as arid, the cultivars have shown that moderate watering is needed during the dry season if maximum flower production is to be enjoyed. Oddly, plumerias also thrive and flower abundantly in areas of very heavy rainfall as long as drainage is excellent. Plumeria displays moderate tolerance to wind and salt. Used as a striking color accent singly or in groves, it is also the source of one of Hawai'i's most treasured leis. Smaller-flowered cultivars are preferred, as they better tolerate handling and are more comfortable for the wearer. Plumerias were admired by the ancient Aztecs, who used the flowers in ceremonials. Virgins of the nobility wore plumeria blossoms in their hair. With other ingredients, a potion containing plumeria sap was drunk as a remedy for fear or faintheartedness. The sap was used in the treatment of wounds and for cutaneous and venereal diseases. In ancient times, commoners who touched plumeria flowers once consecrated for ceremonials were put to death. Currently, garlands made of the flowers are used in the month of May in Taxco (Mexico) to present to the Virgin Mary.

Note: Although detailed information relative to fertilizing, pruning, and plant pests are not usually included in this publication, the recent introduction of the Papaya Mealybug (*Paracoccus marginatus*) has had such a major negative landscape impact on a wide range of popular plants that mention of it seems appropriate. Gardeners must be aware and take steps to control them or avoid their inclusion in the garden. Originating probably in Mexico, the Papaya Mealybug has spread to many mainland areas and was first found on Maui in 2004. It has spread to the Big Island, O'ahu, and Kaua'i. Among the many host plants, there are several of concern to gardeners. These include plumeria, hibiscus, citrus, jatropha, and avocado, in addition to many plants of general economic importance. An infestation on plumeria results in distorted and discolored foliage. Biological control experiments are showing significant success. Avoid chemical treatment that also kills the beneficial insect. At first sign of trouble, use a strong jet of water on infected places twice a week. This will wash away the immature mealybugs. Bag infected material and discard.

P. rubra 'Hilo Beauty'

P. rubra 'Common Yellow'

P. rubra 'Thornton Lilac'

P. rubra 'Daisy Wilcox'

P. rubra 'Kaneohe Sunburst'

P. rubra 'Paul Weissich'

P. rubra 'Kauka Wilder'

Posoqueria latifolia

Needle Flower Tree
Rubiaceae (Coffee Family)

A small tree from Mexico, Peru, and Amazonian Brazil, this species attains 30 feet in height. It is a moderate grower. Its common name derives from the plentiful clusters of long, tubular, fragrant white flowers borne much of the year but more abundantly in spring. The branching habit gives the tree a somewhat vertical shape with a narrow canopy, making it a good subject for a narrow space where it may be used as an accent tree or screen. Pruning to raise its canopy is necessary to produce a shade tree. Use it where its fragrance and flower beauty may be readily experienced. It must have a rich, well-drained, moist soil in full sun or light shade. It fares better when protected from harsh winds. It has a low tolerance of salt.

Psydrax odorata

Alahe'e
Rubiaceae (Coffee Family)

A native tree bearing clusters of highly fragrant white flowers sporadically through the year, Alahe'e will rather slowly attain 30 feet in height. It has shiny dark green foliage. It is drought, wind, and quite salt tolerant. A good selection for a difficult spot in the landscape, Alahe'e will grow in almost any well-drained soil. Its slow rate of growth is enhanced by regular feeding and watering. Minor pruning will assist in producing a tree form. Nurseries specializing in native plants offer good-sized specimens in tubs. Formerly, Hawaiians used its very hard wood to make long digging sticks. Its flowers and foliage are valued by the lei maker. Use it as a fine foliage accent and a source of lei flowers or as a screen, hedge, or windbreak.

Pterocarpus rohrii

Mexican Pterocarpus (NP)
Fabaceae (Bean Family)

This is an amazingly variable species. It is found from dry parts of southern Mexico south through Central America, Brazil, and into Peru and Bolivia in both low and heavy rainfall areas. It is described as varying from 20 to 90 feet in height. The local specimen is a very slow grower and has not reached 20 feet in height after many years. In spring it bears an abundance of golden yellow flowers. It is wind and drought tolerant but not tolerant of salt. Plant it in full sun in a well-drained soil. It makes an excellent small shade tree and a strong color accent.

Punica granatum

Pomegranate

Punicaceae (Pomegranate Family)

Native to hot, dry areas of the orient, Iran, and Arabia, pomegranate is one of man's oldest cultivated plants. Reaching 25 feet in height rather slowly, it is an excellent choice for a problem area. Plant it in deep, well-drained soil. It tolerates both acid and alkalai soils, drought, and wind. Minimal pruning will enhance its tree shape. It bears large, bright red flowers and fruit. A sterile form with double flowers is available, as are several dwarf forms. In its native areas, roots, leaves, fruits, and flowers are a source of medicine, while in ancient Egypt, wine was made from the fruit. A popular drink, grenadine, is produced from the fruit, while a red dye famous for coloring Moroccan leather is another pomegranate product. It will also stain clothing. The pomegranate is the national floral emblem of Spain. In the landscape, use it as a flower color accent, for its shade, and for its edible fruit. It may be espaliered easily or planted against a wall for its silhouette and form.

Quassia amara

Amargo Bark

Simaroubaceae (Torchwood Family)

Growing slowly to 20 feet in height, this colorful ever-green tree from tropical South America bears bright red blossoms and attractive, large, dark green leaves veined in red. It is a slow grower and requires a good, open, moist soil in a lightly shaded location. It has no tolerance of heat, drought, or salt. Use it in a small space where its unusual foliage and color may be enjoyed. It is a good doorway specimen or general color accent. In its native areas, it has many medicinal applications.

Rhus sandwicensis

Neleau, Neneleau (P?)
Anacardiaceae (Cashew Family)

An endemic species reaching 25 feet in height, this tree carries attractive foliage, frequently red when immature. It is a moderate grower in good, rich, well-drained soils but may also be seen growing on damp, rocky road cuts.

It prefers areas of high rainfall, although it responds to regular watering in drier environments. Neleau displays minimal drought tolerance. Due to its tendency to produce root suckers, it should be planted in a contained area. It fares best in full sun and is a moderate grower. Use Neleau as a shade tree or a color and textural accent tree where its foliage may be appreciated.

Saraca declinata

Red Saraca (N)
Fabaceae (Bean Family)

Bearing showy clusters of orange-red flowers in winter through spring and sporadically throughout the warm months, this tree from Java and Sumatra reaches 30 feet in height, although some authors indicate a greater height. New foliage is pendant, colored whitish-lavender turning green, and more upright upon maturity. Plant it in full sun, in good soil, and in a place sheltered from wind. It requires regular watering for best results and is a moderate grower. It is a fine small shade tree and an excellent color accent in the landscape. *Saraca diversifolia*, also pictured, is similar in all respects to the Red Saraca but produces orange-yellow flowers. Another closely related species but not pictured is *S. palembanica*, or Orange Saraca, native to the tropical rain forest at the eastern end of the island of Sumatra. It bears large clusters of golden yellow-orange blossoms with red centers. Its requirements are the same as for the Red Saraca, and all are beautiful color accents in any garden.

S. diversifolia

Saraca indica
Shasoka Tree (N)
Fabaceae (Bean Family)

A tree reaching 30 feet in height, Shasoka is native to the moist tropics of southeastern Asia, Sumatra, and Java. The inflorescence is yellow to red and orange-red. Plant this beautiful small tree in full sun or light shade, in good soil, and in a place sheltered from wind. It must have regular watering and good drainage. There is a long-standing nomenclatural problem: *S. indica*, locally known for decades as the Sorrowless Tree under which the Buddha was born, is actually a different species. The true Sorrowless Tree, or Asoka, is *Saraca asoca*, native to India, Sri Lanka, and Myanmar. In any event, both species are beautiful and highly useful in the landscape as color accents. Both have the same horticultural requirements. Both are moderate growers.

Saraca thaipingensis
Yellow Saraca (N)
Fabaceae (Bean Family)

The Yellow Saraca hails from Thailand, Burma, the Malay Peninsula, and Java. It grows to 30 feet in height and is spectacular when in full bloom. Flowers are clustered and are a golden yellow. They may be seen in winter and spring and sporadically at other times. It requires the same garden care as its cousins above and is an excellent color accent in the landscape. It requires some protection from strong winds and must have generous, regular watering.

Scaevola taccada

Beach Naupaka
Goodeniaceae (Naupaka Family)

The common native Beach Naupaka grows to 10 feet in height. This form from tropical South Pacific islands reaches 20 feet in height producing a dense canopy. Like the species, it will grow in any well-drained soil and pure sand. It is tolerant of wind, salt, drought, and heat. It is a valuable addition to the beach garden or xeriscape as a screen or windbreak and with mimimal pruning can be maintained as a small shade tree. Plant it in full sun. It is a moderate grower.

Schefflera elegantissima

False Aralia
Araliaceae (Panax Family)

This New Caledonian evergreen tree reaches 25 feet in height, although some references indicate a greater height. It requires good, well-drained soil and regular watering. It is a moderate grower in full sun or light shade. Juvenile growth produces narrow, serrated leaflets, while mature leaflets are broad. This may cause identification confusion. Use this beautiful small tree for its shade-giving canopy and as a foliar accent.

Senna surratensis

Evaluate (HPWRA)

Scrambled Eggs, Kolomona (N) (P)
Fabaceae (Bean Family)

A fast-growing evergreen tree from dry parts of tropical Asia, Australia, and Polynesia, this species reaches 20 feet in height. It bears masses of bright yellow flowers throughout the year. They may be used by the lei maker. It is highly drought tolerant, wind tolerant, and quite salt-air tolerant and thrives in any well-drained soil. For best performance, plant it in full sun. It is used as a small shade tree, screen, or hedge or as a bright color accent. It is a good selection for the xeriscape.

Sesbania grandiflora

Vegetable Hummingbird, Sesban, ʻŌhai Keʻokeʻo (N)
Fabaceae (Bean Family)

Native to tropical Asia, this rapid-growing small tree reaches 30 feet and, under ideal conditions, a little more in height. It flowers all year, bearing large white flowers. There are rosy-pink flowered forms. Leaves are pubescent and of a pleasant gray-green. Its bark is furrowed and corky. All parts of the tree are useful: Flowers may be battered and fried, while tender young leaves and immature seed pods may be eaten fresh in salads or added to soups and curries. Other parts of the tree are a source of fiber, gums, a dye, and medicine. The production of seed pods is yearlong. If they are not harvested for their edible qualities, they may become visually unattractive. The tree will grow in any well-drained soil in full sun and shows a high tolerance of drought and wind and a moderate tolerance of salt. Use it in the landscape for its edible qualities, for its good shade, and, in the pinkish-rose flowered form, as a color accent.

Stemmadenia litoralis

Lechoso
Apocynaceae (Dogbane Family)

Native to Central America, Lechoso is prized for its plentiful, pure white flowers and handsome foliage. It is a moderate grower, thriving in almost any well-drained soil, and it reaches 20 feet in height. It requires regular watering for optimal results. It does not show tolerance to drought, wind, or salt. Use it as a bright accent against a dark wall or as a good shade tree. It is evergreen and produces its fragrant white flowers throughout the year.

Tabebuia aurea

Silver Trumpet Tree
Bignoniaceae (Catalpa Family)

This popular Brazilian tree usually reaches 30 feet in height and under ideal conditions may become slightly taller. Flower color is variable, ranging from golden yellow to pale yellow. They are borne in late spring and summer. Foliage varies from gray-green to silver-green, borne in a rounded canopy. It will grow rather rapidly in almost any well-drained soil. Plant it in full sun. It has good drought tolerance and moderate wind tolerance. It is a good selection for the xeriscape.

Tabebuia berteroi

Hispaniolan Rosy Trumpet Tree
Bignoniaceae (Catalpa Family)

This species from the Island of Hispaniola in the Caribbean reaches 30 feet in height and tends to be somewhat columnar in shape. As its name suggests, it bears light pink flowers most of the year. It grows rather rapidly, thriving in almost any well-drained soil. It is moderately wind and drought tolerant. It needs full sun.

Tecoma stans

H (HPWRA)

Yellow Elder Tree
Bignoniaceae (Catalpa Family)

Reaching 30 feet in height, this tree from several of the most southern United States and south through Central America and the West Indies to northern Argentina is prized for its abundant crop of bright yellow flowers. It is a moderate grower, requiring a well-drained soil, full sun, and protection from salt winds. It is heat, wind, and moderately drought tolerant and provides a strong color accent in the landscape. It can also be used as a screen or hedge. Pruning is needed to produce a tree shape.

Tetraplasandra oahuensis

'Ohe Mauka
Araliaceae (Panax Family)

Found on all the main islands except Ni'ihau and Kaho'olawe, this endemic tree will grow to 30 feet in height, preferring moist, cooler elevations. It requires a rich, well-drained soil and regular watering. It thrives best in full sun but will tolerate light shade. It is wind tolerant but looks best when given some protection from strong wind. It is not drought or salt-air tolerant. It is prized for its highly attractive foliage, which produces an interesting accent in the garden. It makes a good shade tree or screen.

Thevetia peruviana
H (HPWRA)
Be-Still Tree (P) +
Apocynaceae (Dogbane Family)

A tough tropical American species, the Be-Still Tree grows to 25 feet in height and bears large, bright yellow flowers. Cultivars 'Alba' and 'Aurantiaca' show white and pale orange flowers respectively. It is heat, drought, and wind tolerant, and in addition to its use as a shade tree, it may be used as a windbreak or screen. It is valuable in the xeriscape. Growing moderately rapidly in any well-drained soil in full sun, it makes a colorful accent in the garden. Special caution must be used in handling the Be-Still Tree, as all parts of the plant are toxic. A rare close relative, not pictured, is *Thevetia thevetioides*, which grows to 30 feet in height and bears larger flowers. Its uses and horticultural requirements are similar to those of the Be-Still Tree. All parts of both species are seriously toxic.

Tournefortia argentea

Beach Heliotrope, Tahinu
Boraginaceae (Borage Family)

Growing rapidly to 25 feet in height, this tree from beach areas of tropical Asia and the South Pacific is an excellent selection for the beach garden. It grows in any well-drained soil and in pure sand. It has moderate drought tolerance and shows good salt and wind tolerance. Its canopy is broad. Give it space. Its wood is used in canoe building and for firewood. Parts of the tree are used medicinally to reduce fever. There are Micronesian legends involving this tree.

Uncarina grandidieri

Uncarina
Pedaliaceae (Sesame Family)

Growing to 25 feet in height, this unusual, somewhat succulent Madagascan tree produces abundant yellow flowers most of the year. It is a moderate grower. Although heat tolerant, it is only moderately drought tolerant and should be watered on a regular basis as determined by its response. Plant it in full sun or light shade in a well-drained soil. It provides a good color accent in the landscape and is particularly attractive when backed by small dark green foliage.

Warszewiczia coccinia

Trinidad Pride, Wild Poinsettia
Rubiaceae (Coffee Family)

From high rainfall areas in the Amazon Basin to Peru, Venezuela, Trinidad and Tobago, and Costa Rica, this startling species produces a slender tree 30 feet in height. It performs best in acid, rich, well-drained soils in full sun or light shade. It requires ample watering and benefits by protection from strong winds. Small yellow flowers are accompanied by large, bright scarlet bracts, which are the attractive aspect of this plant. There is a double form, 'David Auyong', discovered in Trinidad and commonly referred to as Double Chaconia, but the persistence of its old brown bracts makes it unattractive. Their removal may be a maintenance burden. Trinidad Pride in full flower, during spring and summer, is a potent color accent in the landscape. It displays a low tolerance to salt. It produces a slender, shade-giving canopy, making it a good choice for planting along a walkway bordering a narrow planting space. It also makes a good screening plant. Its unusual color places it as an excellent candidate for the tropical landscape.

Yucca guatemalensis

Spineless Yucca, Giant Yucca
Agavaceae (Agave Family)

Native to dry parts of Mexico, Spineless Yucca grows to 30 feet in height. Foliage is dark green, long and narrow, and long lasting. Flower clusters borne in spring and fall are white and showy. It has a somewhat columnar shape rather than a wide-spreading canopy. Plant it in full sun in any well-drained soil. It shows good drought and wind tolerance and moderate salt tolerance. The Variegated Giant Yucca bears green leaves with white stripes.

Tailored
Small Trees

In the Glossary of Botanical Terms in *Hortus Third: A Dictionary of Plants Cultivated in the United States and Canada*, a tree is defined as "a woody plant that produces one main trunk and a more or less distinct and elevated crown." A shrub, on the other hand, is defined as "a woody plant that remains relatively low and produces shoots or trunks from the base, not tree-like or with a single trunk; a descriptive term not subject to strict circumscription."

There are many large shrubs that, with a few thoughtful, deft cuts with a clean, sharp pair of garden shears, can be transformed into respectable "tailored" small trees with one or several trunks. Some of these are the most colorful and attractive species available to the gardener in both flower and foliage.

Unhappily, in the authors' opinion, the most prevalent concept of pruning is to behead a large, healthy shrub, reducing it to shapeless stubs, or just as bad, pruning it into a ball shape. In both cases, such brutal treatment gains

nothing. The results are not attractive and, if anything, would not induce the average gardener to attempt to create a tailored tree. These practices have also made it difficult in many instances to locate shrubs-to-trees photo ops that demonstrate the potential. Look for a transplantable specimen that has been pruned minimally—or better, one that has been happily ignored and left to grow in its natural form.

The sketches below suggest how to tailor a large shrub into a small tree. Follow-through pruning will usually be necessary at a declining rate of frequency until heavy, fully matured bark is in place and a sturdy crown is established.

A great advantage of the tailored tree is that large shrubs can be transplanted into the garden at full size with little difficulty and with virtually instant landscape results. Be sure to prune the shrub *before* transplanting.

We recommend the following tailored small trees.

Candidate shrub

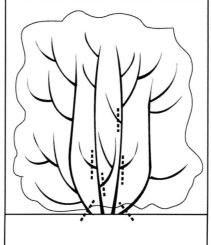

Suggested cuts

Tailored small tree

Acalypha hispida
Chenille Plant
Euphorbiaceae (Euphorbia Family)

Originating in Indonesia, the Chenille Plant will grow to
15 feet in height and is readily shaped into a small tree.
The long, pendant red flowers are borne much of the
year. There is also a white-flowered form (not pictured).
This species appreciates a rich, well-drained soil, regular
watering, and a place in the sun or in light shade. It has
low wind tolerance and little salt tolerance. Its flowering
habit makes this a color accent and a conversation piece.
It is also useful as a screen.

Acalypha wilkesiana

Copperleaf, Jacob's Coat
Euphorbiaceae (Euphorbia Family)

This large shrub, growing to 15 feet in height in either sun or part shade, produces foliage in red and green with yellow variegation. A cultivar, Picotee Acalypha (*Acalypha wilkesiana* 'Picotee'), bears green and white foliage with a white-fringed edge. All show considerable wind and salt wind tolerance and are strong color accents. They may also be used to form a high screen.

A. wilkesiana 'Picotee'

Acca sellowiana

Feijoa
Myrtaceae (Eucalyptus Family)

From southeastern Brazil and Uruguay, this species will reach 15 feet in height. It shows moderate tolerance to wind and drought. It is not salt tolerant. Its tasty fruit, described as a combination of guava and pineapple, is more prolifically borne at cooler elevations. Its fragrant pink flowers are also edible and may be used in salads. Feijoa fares best in a well-drained soil in full sun. In addition to providing a tailored tree, it can also be used as a screen or hedge.

Aglaia odorata

Chinese Rice Flower, Mei-sui-lan
Meliaceae (Mahogany Family)

Areas of Southeast Asia are home to this shrub, which will reach 20 feet in height. It is readily trained into a handsome small tree. It is prized for its fragrant flowers, which are used to scent tea and linens and to wear in women's hair and in leis. Plant this species in a rich, well-watered, and well-drained loam in full sun or light shade. It is partially wind tolerant but is not tolerant of salt or drought. It makes an excellent small shade tree. Plant it where its fragrance may be enjoyed.

Bixa orellana

Lipstick Plant, Achiote
Bixaceae (Annatto Family)

This large tropical American shrub is readily transformed into an attractive tailored tree up to 30 feet in height. Pink flowers seen during late summer to early fall and occasionally sporadically throughout the year are followed by decorative pods colored variously from dull red and bright pink-red to yellow, crowning a dense, rounded canopy. These appear in fall to late fall and are prized by flower arrangers and wreath makers. The pods contain many seeds covered by a powdery red substance that produces a strong dye. In small amounts, it is used in coloring oleomargarine yellow. In former times in the New World, this dye was used to color leather and feathers and was the source of red war paint. Little pruning is required to tailor this useful species.

Bontia daphnoides

Bontia
Myoporaceae (Myoporum Family)

A remarkably tough, large shrub or small tree native to dry areas from the Bahamas, Cuba, and other Caribbean islands to Guiana, Bontia is drought, heat, wind, and salt tolerant. It rather slowly attains 25 feet in height and requires a bit of pruning to realize a small tree shape. Its flowers are insignificant. In addition to its heavy shade-producing canopy, Bontia makes an excellent screen, windbreak, or hedge. Plant it in full sun in any well-drained soil. It is a good candidate for the xeriscape and for the beach garden.

Brunfelsia americana

Lady of the Night, Dama del Noche
Solanaceae (Potato Family)

Native to the West Indies, this species bears creamy white flowers that are strongly fragrant at night. They may be used in lei making. Although only growing to 10 feet in height, it can be pruned into a small tree to shade a walkway or frame an entry. It is moderately wind, heat, and drought tolerant but does not thrive in areas exposed to salt wind. Plant it in full sun in a good, well-drained soil. Because related species produce toxins, it is wise to avoid ingesting any part of this plant.

Brunfelsia australis

Yesterday-Today-and-Tomorrow
Solanaceae (Potato Family)

The strange common name of this attractive species from southern Brazil, Paraguay, and Argentina is derived from its flowering pattern: blue-purple upon opening, blue the following day, and almost white the third day. Flowers are fragrant and may be used in leis. Although usually seen in gardens as a spreading shrub growing rather slowly to 12 feet in height, it can be trained into a small tree and used to line a walkway or frame an entry or garden gate. Plant this color accent in light shade in a rich, well-drained soil. Provide ample, regular watering. Flowering, occurring in late winter to early summer, is more profuse at cooler elevations. Because related species contain toxins, it is wise to avoid ingesting any part of this plant.

Brunfelsia lactea

Vega Blanca, Jazmin del Monte
Solanaceae (Potato Family)

A Puerto Rican native, this shrubby species grows moderately slowly to a height of 20 feet. It requires pruning to produce a tree shape. It bears large white blossoms that slowly turn yellow with age. They are fragrant at night. Its horticultural needs include planting in full sun or light shade in a rich, well-drained soil. It does not show tolerance to heat, drought, or salt but will succeed in areas of light wind. It is a framing species and finds its greatest use in the night garden, planted where its perfume will be appreciated.

Caesalpinia pulcherrima

Dwarf Poinciana, Pride of Barbados, ʻOhai Aliʻi (N) (P) (T)
Fabaceae (Bean Family)

Doing best in hot locations in full sun, this fast-growing, tropical American evergreen shrub is readily pruned to tree form, attaining 15 feet in height. Yellow Dwarf Poinciana (*C. pulcherrima* f. *flava*) and a form with rose-pink flowers, 'Comptonii', are also available. There is also a pale yellow–flowered form. All are heat, drought, wind, and salt tolerant and make significant color statements in the landscape. They are almost ever-flowering and are popular with lei makers. Due to their sharp spines, they can be used to form an effective barrier hedge. Removal of immature seed pods, as in many species, will prolong its flowering.

C. pulcherrima f. *flava*

Calliandra haematocephala
Red Powderpuff, Lehua Haole (N)
Fabaceae (Bean Family)

Originating in Bolivia, this species may be trained into a tree reaching 20 feet in height with a broad canopy to 20 feet in diameter. It produces its brilliant red flowers in fall and winter when planted in a rich, moist soil with good drainage, although it displays a moderate tolerance to drought once established. It has good tolerance to wind and heat but only small tolerance to salt. It flowers best when grown in full sun but will also thrive in light shade. There is a white and a pink flowering form. It is a very useful color accent.

Calliandra surinamensis
Pink Calliandra, Surinamese Stickpea (N)
Fabaceae (Bean Family)

As its name implies, this species originates from northern South America. It may reach 20 feet in height under optimum conditions and can easily be trained into a fine small tree. Its flowers are pink and white and look like a powder puff. Foliage is fine textured. The corky bark makes a good home for epiphytes such as small ferns, orchids, and bromeliads. It thrives in a good, well-drained soil with ample watering. It is another fine color accent.

Calotropis gigantea

**Crown Flower, Giant Milkweed,
Pua Kalaunu (P) + (S) +**

Aesclepiadaceae (Milkweed Family)

Although growing only to 15 feet in height, this tough plant from India and Southeast Asia can be easily trained into a good small tree. It is remarkably tolerant of salt, drought, heat, and wind. It thrives in any well-drained soil and even pure sand. Its bark is corky and furrowed. Flowers are white or lavender and are prized by the lei maker. In India the flower is sacred to Siva. The buds form one of the arrows of Kama, the Indian god of love, who, like Dan Cupid, shoots his arrows into the hearts of mortals. Its attractive, succulent, whitish-grey leaves are the favored food for the caterpillar of the Monarch Butterfly, which in winter may completely defoliate the specimen. It quickly recovers. Plant it in full sun.

Note: Great care should be used in handling any part of the Crown Flower plant, as its milky sap contains a toxic ingredient that irritates the skin and can even be fatal in large doses. It does have medicinal uses, however.

Calotropis procera

Rooster Tree (P) + (S) +
Asclepiadaceae (Milkweed Family)

A slightly smaller relative of the Crown Flower, this species originates from tropical, dry parts of Africa and Asia. It grows to 12 feet in height and is readily pruned into a small tree. Its flowers are purple and white and used by lei makers. Thriving in any well-drained soil, the Rooster Tree is highly drought, heat, wind, and salt tolerant. It must have full sun. Take precautionary actions as described on the preceding page, as the milky sap is toxic. Its growth habit and uses resemble those of its larger cousin, *C. gigantea*.

Carissa macrocarpa

Natal Plum (T)
Apocynaceae (Dogbane Family)

A rapidly growing plant from South Africa, the Natal Plum will reach 20 feet in height. It is heat, drought, wind, and salt tolerant. Pruning turns it into a tough small tree bearing fragrant white flowers year-round, followed by decorative, red, edible fruit. It has a milky white sap that—like that of the fig and papaya—is nontoxic. Preferring full sun, it will also tolerate light shading. Almost any well-drained soil or even pure sand will produce satisfactory results. In addition to its usefulness as a small tree, it may be used to form a barrier planting; its forked thorns are sharp and hard. Cultivars with both green and white and light yellow and white leaves are available.

Cestrum nocturnum

Lady of the Night, Night Cestrum (P)
Solanaceae (Potato Family)

Growing rather quickly to 12 feet in height, this plant has flowers that are highly fragrant at night. It requires pruning to reach a tree shape. It prefers a rich, well-drained soil with regular watering. Plant it upwind where its fragrance will perfume the lanai. This Lady of the Night is from the Caribbean islands, Mexico, and Honduras. It has low tolerance of heat, drought, and salt.

Codiaeum variegatum

Croton

Euphorbiaceae (Euphorbia Family)

Highly variable as to foliage color, size, shape, and ulti-mate height of growth, Croton does have many cultivars that will grow slowly to 25 feet in height. These can be readily seen in older neighborhoods. Croton trans-plants well. Best results are seen when planted in a well-drained, rich soil with regular watering and feeding, although it will withstand moderate drought conditions once established. It is evergreen and thrives in both full sun and light shade. It is readily pruned to a tree form, making a strong color statement in the landscape. It also can be used to make a tall hedge or screen. Croton origi-nates in Melanesia.

Dodonaea viscosa

'A'ali'i

Sapindaceae (Soapberry Family)

An excellent, tough, trainable shrub or small tree growing to 24 feet in height, this native Hawaiian plant is highly tolerant of wind, salt, heat, auto pollutants, and drought. It will thrive in any well-drained soil and is a moderate grower. Its papery fruits may vary from white to red to mahogany, and they are a favorite of the lei maker. Its dense, strong wood was used in old Hawai'i for house building. Use it in the garden as a small shade tree, hedge, wind break, or screen.

Dracaena angustifolia

Narrow-Leaved Dracaena
Agavaceae (Agave Family)

Reaching 18 feet in height, this species is native to the broad tropical area from India and Southeast Asia to Australia and certain Pacific islands. It is a popular landscape subject and may be trained into a tree shape for use in narrow places, shading a pathway, or framing an entry. It thrives in good, moist, but well-drained soils in full sun or light shade. It is easily confused with *D. reflexa* but has foliage bunched together at branch ends. It is moderately wind tolerant but not drought or salt tolerant. A variety, *D. angustifolia* var. *honoriae*, the Yellowback Dracaena, carries leaves with white margins. It originates in the Solomon Islands.

Dracaena reflexa

Mauritius Dracaena
Agavaceae (Agave Family)

The very vertical growth habit of this shrub makes it a candidate for pruning into a useful small tree growing to 12 feet in height. Foliage is dark green, curved downward, and is retained along the branches as long as ample water is applied. It originates on the islands of Reunion and Mauritius in the Indian Ocean. A bright, yellow-bordered leaf form is sold under the name 'Song of India' but is correctly named *D. reflexa* cv 'Variegata'. Other variations are 'Song of Jamaica', showing a yellow stripe down the middle of the leaf, and 'Song of Bangkok', showing a light green stripe down the middle of the leaf. All find good use in narrow places planted in a good soil, well-watered and protected from strong winds. They thrive in both full sun and light shade.

D. reflexa 'Song of India'

D. reflexa 'Song of Bangkok'

D. reflexa 'Song of India'

Duranta erecta
H (HPWRA)
Golden Dewdrop (P)
Verbenaceae (Verbena Family)

Native to the broad area from the southern United
States to Argentina, this useful landscape plant is readily converted into a small tree reaching 20 feet in height.
It flowers abundantly, later producing a heavy crop of
small, golden fruits carried in pendant clusters. Flowers are blue-violet. There is a white-flowered variety,
D. erecta var. *alba*, as well as one with green and white
variegated foliage, 'Variegata', which provides a lumi-
nous quality in the landscape if backlighted by the sun
or night-lighted. The very popular 'Gold' carries small
golden-yellow leaves and lavender-blue flowers, while
'Golden Edge' produces green leaves bordered with
golden-yellow. Its flowers are purple. Another cultivar
is 'Geisha Girl', with dark green foliage and blue and
purple flowers. All may be clipped into formal hedges or
used as a natural hedge, screen, or windbreak. Golden
Dewdrop thrives in most well-drained soils with regular
watering and feeding. It is a moderate grower. It is best
in full sun. It shows good tolerance to wind and heat and
is moderately drought tolerant but not tolerant of salt.
All parts of the plant are toxic.

D. erecta var. *alba*

D. erecta 'Variegata'

D. erecta 'Gold'

D. erecta 'Golden Edge'

D. erecta 'Gold'

D. erecta 'Geisha Girl'

Euphorbia leucocephala

Pascuita, Flor de Niño
Euphorbiaceae (Euphorbia Family)

This tall shrub from cool, moist areas of Central America produces masses of white bracts in late fall, frequently lasting into the Christmas season in the northern hemisphere. It is readily maintained as a small tree, reaching 20 feet in height. Pascuita thrives in any well-drained soil and fares best in full sun when given regular watering and feeding. It is a moderate grower, showing a fair amount of wind tolerance, but it is not tolerant of heat, drought, or salt. Gardeners with sensitive skin should avoid its possibly irritating white sap.

Euphorbia pulcherrima

Poinsettia, Christmas Flower
Euphorbiaceae (Euphorbia Family)

Probably the best-known Christmas flowering plant in the northern hemisphere worldwide, this Mexican and Central American species reaches 15+ feet in height and is readily pruned into a stunning small tree. Traditional bract color is a brilliant red. Poinsettias grow best in a good, well-drained soil and produce their flowers plentifully when regularly watered and fertilized. Its large colored bracts appear in late fall and may last several months. Although somewhat heat, drought, and wind tolerant, flowering is best at cooler elevations. Coastal southern California, with its cold, foggy nights and warm, sunny days produces spectacular flowering. On the Big Island, Kona *mauka* poinsettias show similar growth. Poinsettias fare best with moderate wind protection. Recent research has shown that its white sap is not poisonous.

Ficus microcarpa var. crassifolia
Wax Fig, Taiwan Fig
Moraceae (Mulberry Family)

An Asian species, this fig will reach 12 feet in height. It has a sprawling tendency but with minimal pruning can be trained into a handsome small tree. It is not particular to soil as long as it has good drainage. Although preferring full sun, it will grow in shady areas. Wax Fig is highly salt, wind, and drought tolerant. It also serves well in the xeriscape and the beach garden, where its dark green foliage provides a foil for the usual light-colored foliage typical in both situations.

Ficus septica
Large Leaf Fig
Moraceae (Mulberry Family)

Described as a large shrub or small tree, this ornamental species forms a beautiful tree shape with a little pruning. The leaves are large (17 inches in length, 9 inches across), medium green, and remain on the tree all year. It likes a good, well-drained soil and some protection from heavy winds, as the leaves may be damaged. It is native to northern Australia, Southeast Asia, and India. It shows little heat, drought, salt, or wind tolerance. In addition to providing dense shade, it makes an excellent accent specimen among plants with small dark green foliage or against a wall.

Gardenia brighamii

Nānū
Rubiaceae (Coffee Family)

An endangered Hawaiian species, this rare gardenia is known from only a few rather dry locations in the Islands. It grows slowly to 18 feet in height and requires minor pruning to produce a real tree form. It requires an open soil in full sun. Its rate of growth may be hastened by careful watering and fertilizing. Its plentiful white flowers are fragrant and have long been used in leis. Nānū has become a popular general landscape subject and in the lei garden and is also useful in the xeriscape. Two other rare species—*Gardenia mannii* from Oʻahu and *Gardenia remyi*, found on Kauaʻi, Molokaʻi, Maui, and the Big Island at fairly low elevations—slowly grow to about 40 feet in height. They require a moist but well-drained soil. Both have fragrant white flowers. Unfortunately, both are very difficult to locate in nurseries. All three are placed in the tailored tree category due to their slow growth. They are not pictured.

Gardenia latifolia

Gourri Cup
Rubiaceae (Coffee Family)

Hot, dry areas of southern India and Sri Lanka are home to this slow-growing shrub/tree, which will eventually attain 30 feet in height. Pruning will hasten its developing into a real tree. Flowers are white, fragrant, and plentiful during the summer months. Plant it in full sun in a well-drained soil. Moderate watering will quicken growth. Use it as a small shade tree, hedge, or screen planted where its flowers may be appreciated. Its canopy is dense, providing heavy shade. It is heat, wind, and drought tolerant once well established. In its native areas, it is rare and endangered.

Gardenia latifolia

Gardenia taitensis

Tahitian Gardenia, Tiare, Tiare Tahiti
Rubiaceae (Coffee Family)

Growing moderately rapidly in a sunny location, this excellent landscape subject will attain 20 feet in height, forming a dense canopy providing good shade. It does best in warm coastal areas in any well-drained soil or even sand. It has good wind and salt tolerance. Its large, fragrant white flowers occur plentifully during the warm months. They may be used in cut flower arrangements and in leis.

Gardenia volkensii

Bushveld Gardenia
Rubiaceae (Coffee Family)

Growing slowly to 25 feet in height, this South African gardenia bears a big crop of large, fragrant white flowers. It must have full sun, preferring coastal gardens with high insolation. Pruning is required to develop a tree form. Foliage is dark green and dense. It is wind, heat, and drought tolerant. Flowers are followed by an attractive, woody fruit prized by flower arrangers. While reaching its full stature, it also makes a good screen or windbreak.

Graptophyllum pictum

Caricature Plant

Acanthaceae (Acanth Family)

Probably native to New Guinea, this species is variable as to foliar color, ranging from purple with pink variegation to almost solid purple. Growing moderately rapidly to at least 10 feet in height in either full sun or light shade, the Caricature Plant lends itself well to being trimmed into a small tree shape. It grows best in a good, well-drained loam with regular watering and feeding. It is wind but not salt tolerant. It is an excellent color accent and can be used as a doorway tree or in a small walled garden. It makes a good screen or hedge.

Hamelia patens

Scarlet Bush, Fire Bush
Rubiaceae (Coffee Family)

Native to tropical Mexico and Central America, this ornamental bush will grow to 20 feet in height. As its common names suggest, it bears quantities of orange-red to red flowers much of the year. It bears best in a rich, moist, well-drained soil in full sun. It is a moderate grower. It shows no tolerance of drought or salt but will withstand moderate wind. Scarlet Bush may be easily pruned into a colorful shade tree or used as a major color accent in a hedge or screen.

Hibiscus arnottianus subsp. *immaculatus*

Kokiʻo Keʻokeʻo, Molokaʻi White Hibiscus
Malvaceae (Hibiscus Family)

A rare endemic hibiscus, this species grows moderately rapidly to 12 feet in height and is readily pruned into a tree shape. Its lightly fragrant flowers are pure white without the characteristic colored eye or staminal column shown by other native Hawaiian white hibiscus. Plant it in full sun in a good, well-drained soil. Provide regular watering. Use it as an accent tree, a dooryard framing tree, or even as a hedge or screen. Some protection from strong wind will prevent flower and foliage damage. It shows moderate tolerance to onshore wind.

Hibiscus mutabilis

Cotton Rose, Confederate Rose
Malvaceae (Hibiscus Family)

Growing to 18 feet in height, this species from south China bears many flowers, which open white in the morning and slowly turn to pink by late afternoon. Both single- and double-flowered forms are available. Plant this ornamental shrub-to-tree hibiscus in full sun in a good well-drained soil with ample moisture. It will tolerate moderate wind but not salt. Cotton Rose is a moderately rapid grower. In addition to its shade-giving properties, it can be used in the garden for its color.

Hibiscus rosa-sinensis
Common Red Hibiscus hybrids
Malvaceae (Hibiscus Family)

While the Common Red Hibiscus will grow to 20 feet in height and is easily tailored into a fine small tree, it is its many complex hybrids that provide a wide selection of superior candidates for the gardener. The following extensive listing covers those hybrids that will reach 18 to 20+ feet in height and are readily available: *dark red*: 'Lahaina' and 'Bobby Booth'; *red*: 'Haleakalā'; *orange to yellow*: 'Beach Girl', 'Miss Hawaiian', 'Frank Green', 'Golden Dust', 'Oʻahu Beauty', 'Kīnaʻu Wilder', 'Miss Hawaiʻi', 'New Vasco', 'Liberace', 'Princess Kawānanakoa'; *pink*: 'Double Rainbow', 'America', 'Exquisite', 'Blush'; *wine*: 'Maimai'; *multicolored (orange-red with yellow)*: 'New Rainbow', 'Princess Hanako'; *red center, pink-yellow edge*: 'Charles Niʻi'. Plant these in full sun in a good friable soil and water moderately. They are quite wind resistant and will tolerate considerable salt air. They are somewhat drought tolerant but will defoliate. Regular feeding with a well-balanced fertilizer will promote strong growth and abundant flowering. See notes under *Plumeria rubra* for information concerning the Papaya Mealybug, which also attacks hibiscus.

H. rosa-sinensis 'New Vasco'

H. rosa-sinensis 'Bobby Booth'

H. rosa-sinensis
'Charlie Nii'

H. rosa-sinensis
'Princess Hanako'

Hibiscus schizopetalus

Coral Hibiscus

Malvaceae (Hibiscus Family)

A species from tropical East Africa long cultivated in Hawai'i, Coral Hibiscus grows to 20 feet in height and has been the parent plant for a series of excellent hybrids. The species is very droopy or weeping in shape and is not readily tailored into a small tree. Its hybrids, however, grow more vertically, also to 20 feet in height, and are readily shaped. They may be easily spotted: look for the fringed edge of the petals. Flowers may be pendant and range from deep red and red to yellow with a red throat to pink and white. All are easily transplanted and pruned. The most frequently seen hybrid is 'Pink Butterfly' or 'Pink Waterfall'. It is pictured. There are also several forms with variegated foliage. 'Snowflake', with its strong green and white leaves, is a striking garden accent. All may be used as color accents, screens, and windbreaks. All grow rapidly.

H. schizopetalus 'Snowflake'

H. schizopetalus 'Pink Butterfly'

H. schizopetalus 'Butterfly'

Hibiscus syriacus

Rose of Sharon
Malvaceae (Hibiscus Family)

Growing rather slowly to 15 feet, this large Chinese shrub bears many flowers during much of the year. Flowers—single, semidouble, and double—are seen ranging from white to lavender, rose, pink, and deep pink. Some hybrids may be striped with reddish-pink. It is widely grown in China, Korea, and Japan and is the national flower of Korea. Although growing more sturdily at cooler elevations, Rose of Sharon is highly satisfactory in lowland gardens where it furnishes color, may be used as a hedge or screen, and is readily tailored into a small tree shape. It does best in full sun in a well-drained soil with regular watering, although it will tolerate short periods of drought. It is wind resistant. Use it where its night fragrance may be appreciated.

Ixora finlaysoniana
Siamese White Ixora
Rubiaceae (Coffee Family)

Probably native to Thailand, this tall, slender shrub is easily shaped into a small tree. It will reach 20 feet in height. Clusters of white flowers are borne throughout the year. Planting in full sun or light shade in a well-drained soil with regular watering will produce excellent results. It is a rather slow grower. It is moderately tolerant of wind and drought but shows little tolerance of salt.

Ixora hookeri
Fragrant Ixora
Rubiaceae (Coffee Family)

Growing to 18 feet in height, this large shrub from Madagascar is readily trained into a good tree form. Its long, slender tubular flowers are fragrant. It requires good soil with ample watering. Plant it in full sun for best flowering. It is somewhat wind tolerant but neither drought nor salt tolerant. Fragrant Ixora is a moderate grower.

Ixora spp.

Ixora
Rubiaceae (Coffee Family)

There are several selections from this highly ornamental genus that, with judicious pruning, can become valuable, colorful small trees. Super King Ixora (*Ixora casei* 'Super King') grows to 12 feet or more in height, bearing large clusters of bright red flowers. It is native to the Caroline Islands in the Western Pacific. Nora Grant Ixora (*Ixora chinensis* 'Nora Grant') is similar to Super King Ixora but carries large clusters of coral-pink flowers. It is from tropical China south to the Malay Peninsula and will also grow to 12 feet or more. Red Ixora (*Ixora coccinea*) from Sri Lanka and southern India bears clusters of flowers ranging from white through yellow, pink, and red. All will develop sturdy trunks attaining 12 feet or more in height. All prefer full sun. They thrive in a well-drained soil with regular watering and feeding. They are wind resistant, moderately salt wind tolerant, but suffer under dry conditions. All make excellent hedges and screens.

I. casei 'Super King'

I. chinensis 'Nora Grant'

I. chinensis 'Nora Grant'

Jatropha aconitifolia

Chaya (P)
Euphorbiaceae (Euphorbia Family)

Native to Mexico and Central America, this useful species requires little pruning to achieve a tree form up to 20 feet in height. Chaya was known to the Aztecs and valued for its medicinal properties, although its sap is poisonous. Tender new leaves are edible when cooked, providing significant amounts of vitamin C and iron. In Hawai'i, young stems up to an inch in diameter are peeled, removing all sap-containing material, and eaten raw or cooked. Its ornamental leaves form a rounded canopy. Plant Chaya in good, well-drained, moist soil in full sun. It is wind tolerant and moderately drought tolerant. In the landscape, use it as a handsome foliar accent tree or as part of the edible garden.

Ligustrum japonicum
Evaluate (HPWRA)

Japanese Privet (P)
Oleaceae (Olive Family)

This Japanese evergreen shrub growing to 15 feet in height is usually seen as a dense shrub. It can be easily trained into a fine, tough small tree that tolerates a wide range of soil conditions, even sand, and is tolerant of strong wind and salt spray. White flowers appear in the spring. A cultivar, *L. japonicum* 'Rotundifolium', has more compact growth, with dark green, rounded foliage, and is equally good as a small tree. These are also valued in the landscape as hedges, screens, and windbreaks. Several species of Ligustrum have proven toxic qualities. It is prudent to assume that the Japanese Privet is also toxic.

Lysiloma thornberi

Feather Bush (N)
Fabaceae (Bean Family)

From warm, dry parts of the southern United States, this species attaining 15 feet in height is readily trained into a small tree. It is highly heat and drought tolerant and has good wind and salt tolerance. It thrives in a well-drained soil in full sun. Use it as a small shade tree where a light shade is desired. The fine foliage of Feather Bush provides an interesting accent among other shrubs and trees with dark green, large foliage. It is a moderate grower.

Malvaviscus penduliflorus

Turk's Cap, Firecracker Hibiscus, Aloalo Pahūpahū
Malvaceae (Hibiscus Family)

A tropical American evergreen species reaching 15 feet in height, Turk's Cap may be easily pruned into a small tree. Flowers, appearing throughout the year, are red, pink, or white and are used by the lei maker. It is a moderate grower. Plant it for best results in a good, well-drained soil in full sun. It likes regular watering. It is thought by some botanists that the Turk's Cap commonly seen in local gardens is a cultigen derived from a species found in southern Mexico: *Malvaviscus arboreus* var. *arboreus*. In any event, it is a very useful plant in the landscape, tolerating heat, some drought and wind, but not salt exposure.

Morinda citrifolia

H (HPWRA)

Noni, Indian Mulberry
Rubiaceae (Coffee Family)

Noni is an extremely tough, large shrub that is readily pruned into a small tree shape. Originating in Southeast Asia, it is a moderate grower and will reach 15 feet in height. It is highly tolerant of wind, heat, drought, and salt. It will grow in any well-drained soil and in *pāhoehoe* and *ʻaʻā*. It makes a fine shade tree, its large leaves casting a dense shade. Or it may be used as a hedge or windbreak. Its mature fruit, however, emit a foul odor. Either remove all immature fruit or plant Noni downwind, keeping your neighbor in mind. A variety from Fiji, *M. citrifolia* var. *podownwindtteri*, bears variegated foliage but is not wind, heat, or salt tolerant. It can be pruned into a small tree, providing a strong foliage accent.

Murraya koenigii
Curry Leaf Tree
Rutaceae (Citrus Family)

An attractive small tree up to 10 feet in height, this Indian and Sri Lankan species bears clusters of fragrant white flowers at branch tips in early spring. Foliage is ornamental. This is a widely cultivated tree for its pungent, aromatic fresh leaves—called Karripak (India) and Karapincha (Sri Lanka)—used for flavoring curries. The plant also has medicinal properties. Plant it in full sun in a light, rich, well-drained soil. Water moderately. It does not like wet feet. It is wind and partially drought tolerant. There is also an Indonesian variety with larger leaves and similar uses.

Murraya paniculata
Evaluate (HPWRA)

Mock Orange, Chinese Box, Alahe'e Haole
Rutaceae (Citrus Family)

This large evergreen shrub from India and east to the Philippines will grow to 25 feet in height and is readily pruned into a tree form. Dark green foliage and fragrant white flowers mark this species as an excellent landscape material. Flowering may be induced by withholding water and then applying water generously. It is wind tolerant but has only fair tolerance to drought and salt. A rich, well-drained soil with regular watering produces best growth. It prefers full sun but will accept a lightly shaded site. Flowers and foliage are used to make garlands. In India, Hindus use the flowers in religious ceremonies, especially in the worship of Krishna and Durga. Its very hard wood has been used in wood engraving, for tool handles, and for walking sticks. Unhappily, the flowers cause an allergic reaction similar to hay fever in susceptible persons.

Mussaenda erythrophylla

Ashanti Blood
Rubiaceae (Coffee Family)

Reaching 30 feet or more in height, this colorful tropical West African species requires frequent pruning to counteract its climbing tendency. It may also be used to cover an arbor and will present a brilliant color accent if espaliered or used to cover a fence. One expanded calyx lobe is a strong red. It flowers most of the year. Ashanti Blood grows well in a rich, well-watered, but well-drained soil. Plant it in full sun. It will tolerate a moderate amount of wind but not drought or salt.

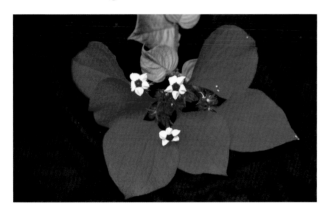

Mussaenda erythrophylla 'Doña Trining'

Doña Trining Mussaenda
Rubiaceae (Coffee Family)

A cultivar of *Mussaenda erythrophylla*, this variety can be pruned into a 15-foot small tree, providing a colorful accent or low screen much of the year. Cultural directions and requirements are the same as for *Mussaenda erythrophylla*.

Mussaenda philippica

Philippines Mussaenda
Rubiaceae (Coffee Family)

This species is found throughout the Philippines and bears flowers with but one white petaloid. It is a moderate grower, reaching 15 feet in height, and it is deciduous during the winter months. It thrives in full sun in a rich, well-drained, moist soil. See also *M. philippica* var. *aurorae* and cultivars.

Mussaenda philippica var. *aurorae*

Mussaenda Doña Aurora
Rubiaceae (Coffee Family)

Native to the area near Mount Makiling, this rare variety was later named Mussaenda Doña Aurora. This variant has all five of its white sepals or calyx lobes fully expanded, forming showy masses of white inflorescences. Height and cultural requirements are the same as those for *M. philippica*.

The Philippine cultivars: Shortly after the close of World War II, plant breeders at the University of the Philippines at Los Baños began highly successful work involving *M. philippica* var. *aurorae*, *M. philippica* forma *philippica*, and the African *M. erythrophylla*. A number of highly landscape-worthy hybrids were developed with colors ranging from white to dark red. In general, they were named after the wives of presidents of the Philippines, although one was named for Queen Sirikit of Thailand, one for the legendary goddess of Mount Makaling, and others for the heroine of a famous book, Maria Clara, and for Filipino ladies of outstanding beauty, poise, and intelligence. They provide excellent subjects for the tailored tree, growing to 10–15 feet in height, preferring a rich, well-drained soil, full sun, and ample watering. They are leafless during the winter months and begin refoliating and flowering in late spring, lasting on through the warm months.

Following are additional selections from the long list of Mussaenda hybrids, indicating the range of colors and forms available: 'Doña Alicia'; 'Doña Leonila'; 'Doña Luz'; 'Magsaysay'; 'Maria Makaling'; 'Doña Paciencia'; and 'Queen Sirikit'.

Mussaenda 'Doña Alicia'

Mussaenda 'Doña Luz'

Mussaenda 'Doña Alicia'

Mussaenda 'Magsaysay'

Mussaenda 'Doña Leonila'

Mussaenda 'Maria Makaling'

Mussaenda 'Doña Luz'

Mussaenda 'Doña Paciencia'

Mussaenda 'Queen Sirikit'

Nerium oleander

Oleander, Common Oleander, 'Oliana (P)+ (S)+
Apocynaceae (Dogbane Family)

This highly drought-, heat-, and wind-tolerant plant grows to 30 feet in height. Oleander shows good salt-air tolerance and tolerance of air pollution caused by traffic. It is seen in southern California and Mediterranean Europe as a street tree, although basal suckering must be regularly cut back, posing a maintenance cost. Planted in full sun, it will grow well in almost any well-drained soil. Highly variable, there are cultivars that display flowers ranging from white through pink, rose, red, salmon, and pale yellow. There are double flowers and those with variegated foliage. There are dwarf cultivars. Fragrance varies from strong to mild. Flowers are borne on new wood, so top pruning is inadvisable. Numerous large, new suckers arise from ground level annually. Retain several of these and remove an equal number of old wood canes, creating an alternating collection of new tree trunks that will produce maximum flower power. This plant is good in the xeriscape and in beach gardens away from direct salt spray. Use Oleander as a small tree, a tough windbreak, a dense screen, or even potted or tubbed on a hot, windswept deck or lanai. It tolerates abuse and is almost indestructible. It is the plant for the nongardener. All parts of Oleander are highly poisonous. Take great care in handling. Avoid burning, as the smoke is toxic. Oleander is native to the very broad area from the Mediterranean eastward to China. It tolerates a range of temperatures, from light freezing to those of the moist tropics.

Pittosporum tobira

Evaluate (HPWRA)

Japanese Pittosporum, Tobira
Pittosporaceae (Pittosporum Family)

Growing slowly to 25 feet in height, this large shrub from Japan and China is a good subject for creative cutting toward forming a small tree. It is tough, has good wind, salt, and drought tolerance, and will thrive in almost any well-drained soil. It prefers full sun but will perform in light shade. It does not fare well in sand. A variety, *Pittosporum tobira* 'Variegata', is available with grey-green foliage edged with white. These plants are not known to flower at lower elevations in Hawai'i. It is a moderate grower.

Pseuderanthemum carruthersii

False Eranthemum

Acanthaceae (Acanth Family)

The highly colorful foliage of two False Eranthemum varieties catches the eye in any garden situation. Purple False Eranthemum (*P. carruthersii* var. *atropurpureum*) displays foliage variegated with purple, pink, and green. Variegated False Eranthemum (*P. carruthersii* var. *variegatum*) shows dark green foliage splotched with grey-green and yellow. They thrive in full sun and part shade. Plant these varieties in a good, well-drained soil and water regularly. All are moderately tolerant of salt wind and minor drought once established. They will attain 10 feet in height and are easily pruned into a small tree form. Excellent color accents, they may also serve as hedges, screens, and windbreaks.

Rhaphiolepis indica

Indian Hawthorn
Rosaceae (Rose Family)

Slowly reaching 10 feet in height, this evergreen shrub from tropical China is well considered as a subject for pruning into a small tree. Growing in full sun in a well-drained soil, it shows good wind tolerance and fair tolerance to drought and salt. It produces white flowers flushed with pink, followed by blackish-purple fruit. It will tolerate light shade. Use it as an entryway accent or screen. It also finds use as a hedge, screen, or windbreak.

Rhaphiolepis umbellata
var. *integerrima*

Yeddo Hawthorn
Rosaceae (Rose Family)

A Japanese evergreen shrub, this species under good garden conditions will reach over 10 feet in height and is easily pruned into a small tree shape. It has good salt, wind, and drought tolerance. Attractive purple-black fruits follow its white flowers, which are seen in winter. Plant it in a well-drained soil in full sun for best results, although it will tolerate light shade. It also finds use in the garden as a screen, hedge, or windbreak.

Rondeletia odorata

Rondeletia
Rubiaceae (Coffee Family)

Although usually placed in the up-to-6-feet category, under ideal conditions specimens may be found reaching 10 feet in height. It is readily pruned into a small tree shape. A native of Cuba and Panama, it flowers much of the year. It is wind tolerant and somewhat drought tolerant once well established. It is not salt tolerant. Plant it in full sun in a well-drained soil. Use Rondeletia as a spectacular color accent or as a small tree bordering a walkway or against a dark wall. It may be used to create a colorful hedge or screen. In spite of its name, its flowers are not fragrant.

Sambucus mexicana var. *bipinnata*

Mexican Elder
Caprifoliaceae (Honeysuckle Family)

Easily grown in any well-drained soil, this rapidly growing shrub up to 30 feet in height is easily trained into a tough small tree. Broad clusters of small white flowers appear much of the year. Care must be taken to plant Mexican Elder in a contained area to prevent wide-spreading roots that produce new shoots and eventually a "clump" rather than a tree. It can, in this way, become invasive. Elder is a form of a Central American species of similar character. It is a candidate for the planter box, where it cannot spread. It is wind tolerant but cannot tolerate drought and salt. Its handsome foliage is a good foil for other plants with large, dark green leaves.

Solanum wrightii

Potato Tree
Solanaceae (Potato Family)

South America is the original home of this ornamental species, which grows fairly rapidly to 15 feet in height. It is readily trainable into a small tree form. It is prized for its large flowers, which open purplish-blue or blue, turning white with maturity, much as its cousin, *Brunfelsia australis*. Flowering is more profuse in cooler areas. Plant it in full sun in a rich, moist, but well-drained soil and protect from strong winds. It is neither drought nor salt tolerant.

Tabernaemontana divaricata

Crepe Jasmine, Crepe Gardenia, Paper Gardenia
Apocynaceae (Dogbane Family)

From northern India and eastward to northern Thailand and southwestern China, this beautiful shrub may grow to 15 feet in height and, with a bit of shaping, has been very successfully used as a small tree. It is readily pruned. Its plentiful flowers are pure white with a yellow throat, fragrant at night, and produced throughout the year. Its wood is fragrant and may be used as incense. Crepe Jasmine takes to almost any well-drained soil in full sun or part shade and appreciates regular watering, although when well established it tolerates a fair amount of drought and wind. It is not tolerant of salts. A double-flowered form, *T. divaricata* 'Flore Pleno' (Butterfly Gardenia), also makes an attractive small tree. It bears larger, dark green, shiny foliage. Both may be used in the garden for hedging and screening.

Tabernaemontana pandacaqi
Small Flowered Crepe Jasmine
Apocynaceae (Dogbane Family)

Growing to 20 feet in height with an equal canopy, this is an evergreen tree from the Philippines, Southeast Asia, Indonesia, Melanesia, and south to Australia. One reference, however, attributes twice that height in growth, which has not been experienced locally. It blooms primarily in summer but its white, somewhat fringed flowers may be seen sporadically throughout the year. Flowers are considerably smaller than those of its Crepe Jasmine cousin but are carried in dense clusters. It requires a moist, well-drained soil in full sun or light shade. It is not wind tolerant and should be given some protection. It is neither drought nor salt tolerant. Use it as a pruned-up shade tree or as a screen or hedge.

Tabernaemontana subglobosa

Philippine Crepe Gardenia

Apocynaceae (Dogbane Family)

A delicate, beautiful, large shrub from the Philippines, this species will attain 15 feet in height with an equal canopy. Very little pruning is needed to produce a tree shape. It bears small, white, pinwheel-shaped flowers abundantly in the warm months and may flower lightly at other times. The flowers are followed by attractive orange, paired fruits. Plant it in full sun in a moist, friable soil with good drainage. It likes moisture. It is somewhat wind tolerant but shows no tolerance to drought or salt. Use it as a graceful accent, small shade tree, or even as a screen.

Thunbergia erecta

Bush Thunbergia, King's Mantle

Acanthaceae (Acanth Family)

An evergreen shrub slowly reaching 15 feet in height, this African native provides a colorful candidate for the shrub-to-tree list. Its blue-purple flowers are seen much of the year. Give it a moist, well-drained soil in full sun or light shade. It shows moderate tolerance of wind, drought (once well established), and salt air. A white-flowering form, *T. erecta* 'Alba', White Bush Thunbergia, is also available.

Vitex trifolia

Blue Vitex

Verbenaceae (Verbena Family)

Blue Vitex is native to the broad area from eastern South Africa to Asia, Australia, and the Pacific. It rapidly reaches 20 feet in height, producing a sprawling shrub that is commonly seen as a hedge but easily pruned and maintained as a small tree. Some people report an allergic reaction as a result of pruning. Before planting Blue Vitex, find out if you are one of those people. Its aromatic foliage is grey-green and flowers are blue to deep blue. It grows readily in poor soil, good soil, and sand and is tolerant of heat, drought, wind, and salt. It must have good drainage. Use it as a small tree, a hedge, or a windbreak. It is a good choice for the xeriscape and the beach garden. Quite similar is *V. trifolia* var. *subtrisecta*, which bears both simple and trifoliate leaves on the same plant and is also frequently used in local gardens. Also popular is *V. trifolia* 'Variegata', bearing white-margined leaves. Both have the same uses in the landscape as Blue Vitex. There is also a variety with leaves whose undersides are an attractive purplish color, possibly *Vitex trifolia* 'Purpurea', sometimes listed in the trade as Fascination Vitex. It is native from Asia to Australia and has the same requirements and uses as those listed above. It reaches 25 feet in height. Vitex nomenclature is somewhat confusing. This does not detract from their considerable usefulness.

Appendix A: Hawai'i-Pacific Weed Risk Assessment Project

The Hawai'i-Pacific Weed Risk Assessment Project (HPWRA) is a joint project of the University of Hawai'i and Kaulunani Urban and Community Forestry, a program of the State of Hawai'i Department of Land and Natural Resources, Division of Forestry and Wildlife, and the U.S. Department of Agriculture Forest Service. The intent of the project is to identify plants that pose a high weed risk in Hawai'i. There are four basic designations:

1. L and L (Hawai'i) indicates that species are not currently recognized as invasive. These designations are not included in this volume's species listings.
2. H (Hawai'i) indicates that the listed species is "documented to cause significant ecological or economic harm to Hawai'i." These species are not recommended by the authors for planting, even though they are commonly used landscape species. They include *Psidium cattleianum* (Strawberry Guava), *Psidium guajava* (Common Guava), *Schefflera actinophylla* (Octopus Tree), and *Schinus terebinthifolius* (Christmas Berry Tree).
3. H (HPWRA) indicates that the listed species is "likely to be invasive in Hawai'i." This is a prediction, but it lacks in-the-field evaluation and, therefore, it is not yet documented. These species include *Bauhinia monandra* (Pink Bauhinia), *Bauhinia purpurea* (Purple Orchid Tree), *Cinnamomum verum* (Cinnamon Tree), *Clerodendrum quadriloculare* (Starburst), *Coffea arabica* (Arabian Coffee), *Duranta erecta* (Golden Dewdrop), *Eugenia uniflora* (Surinam Cherry), *Ligustrum sinense* (Chinese Privet), *Morinda citrifolia* (Noni), *Tecoma stans* (Yellow Elder), and *Thevetia peruviana* (Be-Still Tree). They are recommended for planting but with the request that if any sign of invasiveness is seen, both the parent plant and all seedlings be destroyed.
4. Several species are in the project's "Evaluate" list and have been included in the text. The "Evaluate" list reflects the lack of important information or the difficulty of assessing them using the project system. They are, however, valuable landscape species and include *Clusia rosea* (Autograph Tree), *Eriobotrya japonica* (Loquat), *Ligustrum japonicum* (Japanese Privet), *Murraya paniculata* (Mock Orange Tree), *Pittosporum tobira* (Japanese Pittosporum), *Pittosporum viridiflorum* (Cape Pittosporum), and *Senna surratensis* (Scrambled Eggs, Kolomona).

Appendix B: Small Trees for Windbreak or Screening

In an effort to expedite the gardener's search for the best selection of a small tree, the two basic groups—"Small Trees" and "Tailored Small Trees"—have been combined in the following lists. Species of Small Trees appear in *italics*, while Tailored Small Trees are in ***bold italics***.

Acalypha hispida
Acalypha wilkesiana
Acca sellowiana
Anacardium occidentale
Averrhoa carambola
Bauhinia hookeri
Bauhinia tomentosa
Bauhinia x blakeana
Bontia daphnoides
Brexia madagascariensis
Callistemon citrinus
Callistemon rigidus
Callistemon viminalis
Calotropis gigantea
Calotropis procera
Cerbera manghas
Chrysobalanus icaco
Cinnamomum verum
Citrus maxima
Citrus x reticulata x C. x 'Tangelo'
Clerodendrum quadriloculare
Clusia rosea
Codiaeum variegatum
Coffea arabicum
Coffea liberica
Colobrina oppositifolia
Cordia lutea
Cordia sebestena
Dodonaea viscosa
Dracaena angustifolia
Dracaena cinnaberi
Dracaena fragrans
Dracaena marginata and cultivars
Duranta erecta and cultivars
Eriobotrya japonica
Eugenia brasiliensis
Eugenia uniflora
Euphorbia cotinifolia
Ficus carica
Ficus microcarpa var. ***crassfolia***

Ficus triangularis
Gardenia brighamii
Gardenia latifolia
Gardenia taitensis
Gardenia volkensii
Graptopetalum pictum
Guaiacum officinalis
Guaiacum sanctum
Haematoxylon campechianum
Hamelia patens
Harpephyllum caffrum
Harpullia pendula
Hibiscus arnottianus subsp.
    immaculatus
Hibiscus arnottianus subsp.
    punaluuensis
Hibiscus hamabo
Hibiscus rosa-sinensis and hybrids
Hibiscus schizopetalus and hybrids
Hibiscus syriacus
Hibiscus waimeae
Ixora finlaysoniana
Ixora spp.
Jatropha integerrima
Lagerstroemia archeriana
Lagerstroemia indica
Lawsonia inermis
Ligustrum japonicum
Ligustrum japonicum 'Rotundifolium'
Ligustrum sinense
Lysiphyllum cunninghamii
Malpighia emarginata
Malvaviscus penduliflorus
Mangifera indica 'Fairchild'
Mangifera indica 'Julia'
Manilkara zapota
Melaleuca bracteata 'Revolution Gold'
Metrosideros polymorpha
Morinda citrifolia
Murraya koenigii

Murraya paniculata
Myoporum sandwicense
Nerium oleander and cultivars
Ochna integerrima
Ochrosia elliptica
Pandanus tectorius
Pittosporum confertiflorum
Pittosporum flocculosum
Pittosporum hosmeri
Pittosporum tobira
Pittosporum viridiflorum
Platycladus orientalis
Plumeria lambertiana
Plumeria obtusa
Plumeria obtusa (Bahamas)
Plumeria obtusa var. *sericifolia*
Plumeria rubra and hybrids
Posoqueria latifolia
Psydrax odorata
Punica granatum
Rhaphiolepis indica
Rhaphiolepis umbellata var.
    integerrima
Rondeletia odorata
Scaevola taccada (Fiji)
Senna surattensis
Tabebuia aurea
Tabebuia berteroi
Tabernaemontana divaricata
Tabernaemontana pandacaqi
Tabernaemontana subglobosa
Tecoma stans
Tetraplasandra oahuensis
Thevetia peruviana
Thevetia thevetioides
Thunbergia erecta
Vitex trifolia
Vitex trifolia 'Purpurea'
Warszewiczia coccinia

Appendix C: Small Trees for Coastal Gardens

Numerals following the species name indicate the zone in which that species persists without severe damage from salt wind or spray. Zone I is the area of the beach garden fully exposed to strong onshore winds; Zone II is the area sheltered by Zone I plantings and/or a structure, if present; Zone III is the garden area sheltered by Zone II plantings. Recommended zones are conservative, assuming regular, windward, strong onshore wind. In leeward areas, most of the Zone II species might be expected to thrive in the Zone I area. (Small Trees are shown in *italics*, Tailored Small Trees in ***bold italics***.)

Acalypha wilkesiana II
Anacardium orientale II
Bontia daphnoides I
Brexia madagascariensis II
Bucida molineti II
Caesalpinia pulcherrima II
Caesalpinia pulcherrima 'Comptonii' II
Caesalpinia pulcherrima f. ***flava*** II
Callistemon citrinus III
Callistemon rigidus III
Callistemon viminalis III
Calotropis gigantea I
Calotropis procera I
Carissa macrocarpa I
Cerbera manghas II
Chrysobalanus icaco I
Clusia rosea I
Codiaeum variegatum II
Cordia lutea II
Cordia sebestena II
Dodonaea viscosa II
Dracaena cinnaberi II
Dracaena draco II
Dracaena marginata and cultivars II
Ficus carica II
Ficus microcarpa var. ***crassifolia*** I
Gardenia taitensis I
Guaiacum officinale III
Guaiacum sanctum III
Guettarda speciosa II
Hibiscus arnottianus subsp. ***immaculatus*** III
Hibiscus arnottianus subsp. *punaluuensis* II
Hibiscus hamabo II
Hibiscus rosa-sinensis and hybrids II
Hibiscus schizopetalus and hybrids II

Ligustrum japonicum II
Ligustrum japonicum cv 'Rotundifolium' II
Lysiloma bahamensis I
Lysiloma thornberi II
Manilkara zapota and cultivars II
Metrosideros polymorpha II
Morinda citrifolia I
Munroidendron racemosum III
Murraya paniculata II
Myoporum sandwicense I
Nerium oleander II
Nolina recurvata II
Ochrosia elliptica II
Pandanus tectorius and cultivars I
Pittosporum tobira I
Pittosporum tobira 'Variegata' I
Platycladus orientalis II
Plumeria lambertiana II
Plumeria obtusa (Bahamas) I
Plumeria obtusa var. *sericifolia* II
Pseuderanthemum carruthersii var. ***atropurpureum*** III
Pseuderanthemum carruthersii var. ***variegatum*** III
Psydrax odorata II
Rhaphiolepis indica II
Rhaphiolepis umbellata var. ***integerrima*** II
Scaevola taccada I
Senna surratensis II
Thevetia peruviana III
Thevetia thevetioides III
Thunbergia erecta III
Tournefortia argentea I
Vitex trifolia I
Vitex trifolia cv 'Variegata' I
Vitex trifolia var. ***subtrisecta*** I
Yucca guatemalensis II

Appendix D: Small Trees with Significant Flowers or Colored Fruit or Foliage

Small Trees are listed in *italics*, Tailored Small Trees in **bold italics**.

Acalypha hispida
Acalypha wilkesiana
Acca sellowiana
Amherstia nobilis
Anacardium occidentale
Archidendron clypearia
Averrhoa carambola
Bauhinia x blakeana
Bauhinia hookeri
Bauhinia tomentosa
Bixa orellana
Bolusanthus speciosus
Brownea coccinea subsp. *capitella*
Brownea coccinea subsp. *coccinea*
Brownea grandiceps
Brownea latifolia
Brownea macrophylla
Brugmansia x candida
Brunfelsia americana
Brunfelsia australis
Brunfelsia densifolia
Brunfelsia lactea
Caesalpinia pulcherrima
Caesalpinia pulcherrima 'Comptonii'
Caesalpinia pulcherrima f. *flava*
Calliandra haematocephala
Calliandra surinamensis
Callistemon citrinus
Callistemon rigidus
Callistemon viminalis
Calotropis gigantea
Calotropis procera
Cassia roxburghii
Cestrum nocturnum
Citrus maxima
Citrus x reticulata x C. x 'Tangelo'
Clerodendrum quadriloculare
Codiaeum variegatum
Coffea arabica
Coffea liberica
Colobrina oppositifolia
Cordia lutea

Cordia sebestena
Diphysa americana
Dodonaea viscosa
Dracaena cinnaberi
Dracaena draco
Dracaena fragrans and cultivars
Dracaena marginata and cultivars
Dracaena reflexa and cultivars
Duranta erecta and cultivars
Erythrina cristi-galli
Eugenia brasiliensis
Eugenia uniflora
Euphorbia cotinifolia
Euphorbia leucocephala
Euphorbia pulcherrima
Gardenia brighamii
Gardenia latifolia
Gardenia mannii
Gardenia remyi
Gardenia taitensis
Graptophyllum pictum
Guaiacum officinalis
Guaiacum sanctum
Hamelia patens
Harpullia pendula
Hibiscus arnottianus subsp.
  immaculatus
Hibiscus arnottianus subsp.
  punaluuensis
Hibiscus clayi
Hibiscus kokio
Hibiscus mutabilis
Hibiscus rosa-sinensis and hybrids
Hibiscus schizopetalus hybrids
Hibiscus syriacus
Hibiscus waimeae
Ipomoea pauciflora
Ixora finlaysoniana
Ixora hookeri
Ixora spp.
Jatropha integerrima
Kokia drynarioides

Kopsia fruticosa
Kopsia pruniformis
Lagerstroemia archeriana
Lagerstroemia indica
Lawsonia inermis
Lysiphyllum cunninghamii
Majidea zanquebarica
Malpighia emarginata
Malvaviscus penduliflorus
Melaleuca bracteata 'Revolution Gold'
Metrosideros polymorpha
Metrosideros tremuloides
Murraya koenigii
Murraya paniculata
Mussaenda erythrophylla
Mussaenda erythrophylla 'Doña
  Trining'
Mussaenda philippica 'Aurorae'
Mussaenda x 'Doña Alicia'
Mussaenda x 'Doña Aurora'
Mussaenda x 'Doña Luz'
Mussaenda x 'Queen Sirikit'
Napoleonaea imperialis
Nerium oleander and cultivars
Ochna integerrima
Ochrosia elliptica
Pandanus tectorius cv 'Baptistii'
Pandanus tectorius cv 'Veitchii'
Pisonia grandis 'Alba'
Plumeria lambertiana
Plumeria obtusa (Bahamas)
Plumeria obtusa var. *sericifolia*
Plumeria pudica
Plumeria rubra and hybrids
Posoqueria latifolia
Pseuderanthemum carruthersii var.
  atropurpureum
Pseuderanthemum carruthersii var.
  variegatum
Psydrax odorata
Pterocarpus rohrii
Punica granatum

Quassia amara
Rhus sandwicensis
Rondeletia odorata
Sambucus mexicana var. **bipinnata**
Saraca declinata
Saraca indica
Saraca palembanica
Saraca thaipingensis
Senna surratensis

Sesbania grandiflora
Solanum wrightii
Stemmadenia litoralis
Tabebuia aurea
Tabebuia berteroi
Tabernaemontana divaricata
Tabernaemontana divaricata 'Flore Pleno'
Tabernaemontana pandacaqi

Tabernaemontana subglobosa
Tecoma stans
Thevetia peruviana
Thevetia thevetioides
Thunbergia erecta
Uncarina grandidieri
Vitex trifolia 'Purpurea'
Warszwiczia coccinia
Yucca guatemalensis

Appendix E: Small Trees with Edible Fruit or Leaves

Small Trees are listed in *italics*, Tailored Small Trees in ***bold italics***.

Acca sellowiana

Anacardium occidentale

Annona x *atemoya*

Annona muricata

Annona squamosa

Averrhoa carambola

Carissa macrocarpa

Chrysobalanus icaco

Cinnamomum verum

Citrus maxima

Citrus reticulata

Citrus x *nobilis* cv 'Temple'

Citrus x *reticulata* x *C.* x Tangelo

Coffea arabicum

Coffea liberica

Eriobotrya japonica

Eugenia brasiliensis

Eugenia uniflora

Ficus carica

Ficus dammaropsis

Harpephyllum caffrum

Jatropha aconitifolia

Malpighia emarginata

Mangifera indica 'Fairchild'

Mangifera indica 'Julie'

Manilkara zapota and cultivars

Morinda citrifolia

Moringa oleifera

Murraya koenigii

Parmentiera aculeata

Phyllanthus acidus

Punica granatum

Sesbania grandiflora

A note about the use of fruit trees in the landscape: do not plant fruit trees unless you intend to harvest the crop. Unpicked fruit will create an odoriferous mess, attract flies and rodents, and constitute a potential slipping/falling hazard. If all ripe fruit cannot be picked, use a ground cover that will enable the gardener to rake up fallen fruit. Avoid placing the tree over paving. Fruit trees are not recommended for planting in public places as they may be considered an attractive nuisance and a source of litigation.

Appendix F: Small Trees for Warm, Dry Environments

Small Trees are listed in *italics*, Tailored Small Trees in ***bold italics***.

Anacardium occidentale
Bauhinia hookeri
Bauhinia tomentosa
Bolusanthus speciosus
Bontia daphnoides
Caesalpinia pulcherrima
Caesalpinia pulcherrima 'Comptonii'
Caesalpinia pulcherrima f. ***flava***
Callistemon citrinus
Callistemon rigidus
Callistemon viminalis
Calotropis gigantea
Calotropis procera
Cassia roxburgii
Chrysobalanus icaco
Citrus x *nobilis* cv 'Temple'
Clusia rosea
Colobrina oppositifolia
Cordia lutea
Cordia sebestena
Crescentia cujete
Diphysa americana
Dodonaea viscosa
Dracaena cinnaberi
Dracaena draco
Dracaena marginata and cultivars

Ficus carica
Ficus microcarpa var. ***crassifolia***
Gardenia brighamii
Gardenia latifolia
Gardenia volkensii
Guaiacum officinale
Guaiacum sanctum
Harpephyllum caffrum
Ipomoea pauciflora
Kokia drynarioides
Lawsonia inermis
Lysiloma bahamensis
Lysiloma thornberi
Lysiphyllum cunninghamii
Malpighia emarginata
Mangifera indica 'Fairchild'
Mangifera indica 'Julie'
Metrosideros polymorpha
Morinda citrifolia
Moringa oleifera
Myporum sandwicense
Nerium oleander and cultivars
Nolina recurvata
Parmentiera aculeata
Pleomele aurea

Pleomele hawaiiensis
Plumeria lambertiana
Plumeria obtusa (Bahamas)
Plumeria obtusa var. *sericifolia*
Plumeria pudica
Plumeria rubra and hybrids
Psydrax odorata
Pittosporum tobira
Pterocarpus rohrii
Punica granatum
Rhaphiolepis indica
Rhaphiolepis umbellata var. ***integerrima***
Rondeletia odorata
Scaevola taccada
Senna surratensis
Sesbania grandiflora
Tabebuia aurea
Tabebuia berteroi
Tecoma stans
Thevetia peruviana
Thevetia thevetioides
Vitex trifolia
Vitex trifolia 'Variegata'
Vitex trifolia var. ***subtrisecta***
Yucca guatemalensis

References

Abbott, Isabella Aiona. 1992. *Laʻau Hawaiʻi*. Bishop Museum Press, Honolulu, HI.

Adams, C. D. 1972. *Flowering Plants of Jamaica*. University of the West Indies, Mona, Jamaica. Robert MacLeho and Co. Ltd.

Allen, Paul H. 1977. *The Rain Forests of Golfo Dulce*. Stanford University Press, Palo Alto, CA.

An Alphabetical List of the Plant Species Cultivated in the Hortus Botanicus Bogoriensis. 1957. Foundation for Nature Research (Botanic Gardens of Indonesia), Pertjetakan Archipel. Bogor, Indonesia.

Bailey Hortorium (Cornell University). 1976. *Hortus Third: A Concise Dictionary of Plants Cultivated in the United States and Canada*. Macmillan, New York.

Barwick, Margaret. 2004. *Tropical and Subtropical Trees: A Worldwide Encyclopaedic Guide*. Timber Press, Portland, OR.

Beentje, H. J. 1994. *Kenya Trees, Shrubs and Lianas*. National Museum of Kenya, Nairobi.

Benthall, A. P. 1933. *The Trees of Calcutta*. Thacker Spink and Co., Calcutta, India.

Blatter, Ethelbert, and Walter Samuel Millard. 1954. *Some Beautiful Indian Trees*. 2nd ed., revised by W. T. Stearn. Bombay Natural History Society, India.

Brandis, Dietrich. 1971. *Indian Trees*. Bishen Singh Mahendra Pal Singh, Dehra Dun.

Brock, John. 1988. *Top End Native Plants*. Pub. by the author, Darwin, Northern Territory, Australia.

———. 1993. *Native Plants of Northern Australia*. Reed Books, Victoria, Australia.

Button, Nathaniel L., and Charles F. Millspaugh. 1920. *The Bahama Flora*. Pub. by the authors, New York.

Codd, L. E. W. 1951. *Trees and Shrubs of the Kruger National Park*. Botanical Survey Memoir No. 26, Department of Agriculture, Division of Botany and Plant Pathology. Union of South Africa Government Printer, Pretoria.

Cooke, Theodore. 1967. *Flora of the Presidency of Bombay*. Vol. 1: *Botanical Survey of India by the Government of India*. S. N. Guha Ray, Calcutta.

Corner, E. J. H. 1952. *Wayside Trees of Malaysia*. 2 vols. Governmental Printing Office, Singapore.

Croat, Thomas B. 1978. *Flora of Barro Colorado Island*. Stanford University Press, Palo Alto, CA.

Dale, Ivan R., and P. J. Greenway. 1961. *Kenya Trees and Shrubs*. Colony and Protectorate of Kenya, Buchanan's Kenya Estates, Ltd., in association with Hatchards, London.

Dassanayake, M. D. 1983. *A Revised Handbook to the Flora of Ceylon*. Pub. for the Smithsonian Institution and the National Science Foundation by Amerind Publishing Co. Pvt. Ltd., New Delhi, India.

Dombeck, Michael P. 2003. The Essential Nature of Urban Forests. *Chicago Tribune*, February 11, 2003.

Du Puy, D. J,. J. N. Labat, R. Rabevohitra, J. F. Villers, J. Bosser, and J. Moat. 2002. *The Leguminosae of Madagascar*. Royal Botanic Garden, Kew, London.

Flores, E. M., and W. A. Martin. n.d. *Diphysa americana*. National Academy of Science, Costa Rica, and the School of Biology, University of Costa Rica.

Grierson, Mary, and Peter S. Green. 1996. *A Hawaiian Florilegium: Botanical Portraits from Paradise*. University of Hawaiʻi Press, Honolulu.

Hillebrand, William. 1888. *Flora of the Hawaiian Islands*. B. Westerman and Co., New York.

Hutchison, J., and J. M. Dalziel, eds. 1968. *Flora of West Tropical Africa*. 2nd ed., rev. by F. N. Hepper. Vol. 3, Part 1: *Crown Agents for Overseas Government*. Millbank, London.

Lantin-Rosario, Teresita. 1998. *Oriental Mussaendas of the Philippines*. University of the Philippines Los Baños, Laguna.

Little, Jim. 2006. *Growing Plumerias in Hawaiʻi*. Mutual Publishing, LLC, Honolulu.

Llamas, Kirsten A. 2003. *Tropical Flowering Plants*. Timber Press, Portland, OR.

Lopez Lillo, Antonio, and José Manuel Sánchez de Lorenzo Cáceres. 2004. *Árboles en España: Manual de Indentificacion*. Ediciones Mundi-Prensa, Madrid.

Lord, Ernest E. 1970. *Shrubs and Trees for Australian Gardens*. Lothian Publishing Co. Pty. Ltd., Melbourne.

Mabberley, D. J. 1997. *The Plant Book*. 2nd ed. Cambridge University Press, UK.

Macmillan, H. F. 1952. *Tropical Planting and Gardening*. 5th ed. Macmillan and Co. Ltd., London.

McCann, Charles. 1959. *100 Beautiful Trees of India*. D. B. Taraprevala Sons and Co., Bombay.

McDonald, Marie A., and Paul R. Weissich. 2003. *Nā Lei Makamae: The Treasured Lei*. University of Hawaiʻi Press, Honolulu.

Menninger, Edwin A. 1964. *Seaside Plants of the World*. Hearthside Press, New York.

Milne, E., and R. M. Polhill, eds. 1968. *Flora of Tropical East Africa (Brexiaceae: B. Verdcourt)*. Crown Agents for Overseas Governments and Administrations.

National Research Council. 1979. *Tropical Legumes: Resources for the Future.* National Academy of Sciences Press, Washington, D.C.

Neal, Marie C. 1965. *In Gardens of Hawaii.* Bernice P. Bishop Museum Special Publication 50. Bishop Museum Press, Honolulu.

Palmer, Eve, and Nora Pitman. 1972. *Trees of South Africa.* 3 vols. A. A. Balkema, Capetown.

Pooley, Elsa. 1994. *Trees of Natal.* Natal Flora Publications Trust, Durban, South Africa.

Rauch, Fred D., and Paul R. Weissich. 2000. *Plants for Tropical Landscapes: A Gardener's Guide.* University of Hawai'i Press, Honolulu.

Rock, Joseph F. 1913. *The Indigenous Trees of the Hawaiian Islands.* Pub. privately, Honolulu.

Rojo, Justo P. 1972. Pterocarpus (Leguminosae-Papilionaceae) Revised for the World. *Phanerogamarum Monographica* 5:38. J. Cramer, Lehre. 119 pages.

Schatz, George E. 2001. *Generic Tree Flora of Madagascar.* Royal Botanic Gardens, Kew, London, and the Missouri Botanical Garden.

Skeete, C. C. 1953. *Garden Book of Barbados.* Department of Science and Agriculture. Bridgetown, Barbados.

Standley, Paul C. 1928. *Flora of the Panama Canal Zone.* Smithsonian Institution, U.S. Government Printing Office, Washington, D.C.

———. 1937. *Flora of Costa Rica.* Publication 392, Field Museum of Natural History, Chicago.

———. 1961. *Trees and Shrubs of Mexico.* Smithsonian Institution Publication 4461, Washington, D.C.

Staples, George W., and Derral R. Herbst. 2005. *A Tropical Garden Flora: Plants Cultivated in the Hawaiian Islands and Other Tropical Places.* Bishop Museum Press, Honolulu.

Sugano, Jari, and Steve Fukuda. 2007. Ways to Control Papaya Mealybug. *Honolulu Advertiser*, November 2, 2007.

Thulin, Mats. 1995. *Flora of Somalia.* Royal Botanic Garden, Kew, London.

Wagner, Warren L., Derral R. Herbst, and S. H. Sohmer. 1990. *Manual of the Flowering Plants of Hawai'i.* 2 vols. Bishop Museum Press and University of Hawai'i Press, Honolulu.

Weakley, Leigh. 1987. *Gardening in the Dry Tropics.* Society for Growing Australian Plants, Townsville, Australia.

Westley, Sidney B., and Mark H. Powell, eds. 1993. Erythrina in the Old and New Worlds. Nitrogen Fixing Tree Research Reports, Special Issue. Pā'ia, Hawai'i.

White, F., F. Dowsett-Lemaire, and J. D. Chapman. 2001. *Evergreen Forests of Malawi.* Royal Botanic Garden, Kew, Cromwell Press, London.

Whitmore, J. C., ed. 1973. *Tree Flora of Malaya: A Manual for Foresters.* Vol. 2. Longman, Malaysia, Kuala Lumpur.

Williamson, Jessie. 1955. *The Useful Plants of Nyasaland.* P. J. Greenway, ed. Government Printer, Zomba, Nyasaland. Reprinted 1975 as *The Useful Plants of Malawi,* University of Malawi, Zomba.

Williamson, Joseph F., and the Editors of Sunset Books and Magazine. 1990. *Sunset Western Garden Book.* Lane Publishing Co., Menlo Park, CA.

Worthington, T. B. 1959. *Ceylon Trees.* Colombo Apothecarie Co. Ltd., Colombo, Sri Lanka.

Plant Name Index

About the Authors

Fred D. Rauch, Ph.D., is emeritus professor of horticulture at the University of Hawai'i, where he served as extension specialist in horticulture for twenty-five years. His interest in ornamental plants began while studying for the B.S. degree in horticulture at Oregon State University. He studied tropical landscape plants during research and instruction in horticulture at Mississippi State University. Among his numerous publications are a comprehensive laboratory manual for use in teaching tropical plant courses in the University of Hawai'i system and *Plants for Tropical Landscapes*, coauthored by Paul Weissich. He was instrumental in the formation of the Landscaping Industry Council of Hawai'i.

Paul R. Weissich, A.S.L.A., is currently a licensed landscape architect whose familiarity with tropical landscape species has resulted in numerous consultant assignments. From 1957 to 1989 he was director of the Honolulu Botanical Gardens, where he expanded the two-garden system from 50 to 650 acres covering four sites of differing ecological situations. He also increased the plant collection to a position of international recognition. Weissich coauthored *Plants for Tropical Landscapes* with Fred Rauch and *Nā Lei Makamae: The Treasured Lei* with Marie McDonald. He also wrote *Majesty II: The Exceptional Trees of Hawaii.*